The Development of Logical Empiricism

By

Joergen Joergensen

VOLUMES I AND II · FOUNDATIONS OF THE UNITY OF SCIENCE

VOLUME II · NUMBER 9

THE UNIVERSITY OF CHICAGO PRESS

International Encyclopedia of Unified Science

Editor-in-Chief   Otto Neurath †

Associate Editors   Rudolf Carnap   Charles Morris

Foundations of the Unity of Science

(Volumes I–II of the Encyclopedia)

Committee of Organization

RUDOLF CARNAP
PHILIPP FRANK
JOERGEN JOERGENSEN

CHARLES W. MORRIS
OTTO NEURATH †
LOUIS ROUGIER

Advisory Committee

NIELS BOHR †
EGON BRUNSWIK †
J. CLAY †
JOHN DEWEY †
FEDERIGO ENRIQUES †
HERBERT FEIGL
CLARK L. HULL †
WALDEMAR KAEMPFFERT †
VICTOR F. LENZEN
JAN LUKASIEWICZ †
WILLIAM M. MALISOFF †

R. VON MISES †
G. MANNOURY †
ERNEST NAGEL
ARNE NESS
HANS REICHENBACH †
ABEL REY †
BERTRAND RUSSELL
L. SUSAN STEBBING †
ALFRED TARSKI
EDWARD C. TOLMAN †
JOSEPH H. WOODGER

† Deceased.

THE UNIVERSITY OF CHICAGO PRESS, CHICAGO & LONDON
The University of Toronto Press, Toronto 5, Canada

Contents:

PAGE

I. THE VIENNA CIRCLE: ITS PROGRAM AND PRESUPPOSITIONS . . . 1
  1. Introductory Remarks 1
  2. The Vienna Circle 2
  3. The Program 3
  4. Predecessors 6
  5. The Positivism of Ernst Mach 7
  6. The Logical Positivism of Bertrand Russell 11
  7. Ludwig Wittgenstein's Logical-philosophical Treatise . . . 17
  8. Rudolf Carnap's Theory of the Constitution of Concepts   28

II. LOGICAL EMPIRICISM: ITS EXPANSION AND ELABORATION . . . 40
  1. Publications, Congresses, and International Connections . . 40
  2. The Berlin Group 48
  3. The Lwow-Warsaw Group 54
  4. Pragmatists and Operationalists 55
  5. The Uppsala School 58
  6. The Münster Group 58
  7. Individuals 59
  8. The Question of the Nature of Philosophy 61
  9. Carnap's Logical Syntax of Language 62
  10. Protocol-Sentences and Substantiations ("Konstatierungen") . 68
  11. Verifiability and Testability 71
  12. Unity of Science and Physicalism 76
  13. Present Tendencies and Tasks 83

NOTES AND BIBLIOGRAPHY 87

POSTSCRIPT. By *Norman M. Martin* 91

The Development of Logical Empiricism

Joergen Joergensen

I. The Vienna Circle: Its Program and Presuppositions

1. Introductory Remarks

In Volume II, No. 8, of this *Encyclopedia* Edgar Zilsel outlined the evolution of empiricism in its broad sense up to the beginning of this century. The present article will continue this history, sketching the development until 1940[1] of the recent form of empiricism generally called "logical empiricism."

It is characteristic of this movement, which may presumably be said to have been the leading movement within the philosophy of the last two or three decades, that it is an expression of a need for clarification of the foundations and meaning of knowledge rather than of a need for justification of a preconceived view; that it attempts to make philosophy scientifically tenable through critical analysis of details rather than to make it universal by vague generalizations and dogmatic construction of systems; and that it is more interested in co-operation among philosophers and between philosophers and investigators in the special sciences than in the advancement of more or less striking individual opinions. What unites its members is, therefore, not so much definite views or dogmas as definite tendencies and endeavors. An evidence of this is the often considerable divergence and lively discussion between its members and the amendments in the fundamental views that have occurred several times in the course of its development. On the other hand, the constant exchange of opinion has led to an increasing convergence toward certain basic principles that have gradually taken shape and that now form the common basis for the further discussion of still unsettled questions. The nature of these fundamental principles will be clarified in the following exposition.

2. The Vienna Circle

The nucleus from which logical empiricism developed was the so-called "Vienna Circle," the origin of which is described by Herbert Feigl, one of its younger members, as follows:

"The Vienna Circle evolved in 1923 out of a seminar led by Professor Moritz Schlick and attended, among other students, by F. Waismann and H. Feigl. Schlick's teaching period in Vienna had begun in 1922, and by 1925 out of this nucleus a Thursday evening discussion group was formed. It is interesting to note that many of the participants were not professional philosophers. Even if some of them taught philosophy, their original fields of study lay in other disciplines. Schlick, for example, had specialized in physics, and his doctor's thesis, written under the guidance of Max Planck in Berlin, concerned a problem in theoretical optics. Among the other active members we may mention: Hans Hahn, mathematician; Otto Neurath, sociologist; Victor Kraft, historian; Felix Kaufmann, lawyer; Kurt Reidemeister, mathematician. An occasional but a most contributive visitor was the Prague physicist, Philipp Frank (now at Harvard). In 1927 and again in 1932 the brilliant Finnish psychologist and philosopher, E. Kaila, was present as an active and critical member of the group. Another visitor from Scandinavia was Å. Petzaell (Göteborg). Among the younger participants were K. Goedel (now at Princeton), T. Radakovic, G. Bergmann, M. Natkin, J. Schaechter, W. Hollitscher, and Rose Rand; and, among the visitors, C. G. Hempel, Berlin; A. E. Blumberg, Baltimore; and A. J. Ayer, Oxford. Among those more loosely affiliated with the group were K. Menger, E. Zilsel, K. Popper, H. Kelsen, L. v. Bertalanffy, Heinrich Gomperz, B. von Juhos.

"The most decisive and rapid development of ideas began in 1926 when Carnap was called to the University of Vienna. His contributions to axiomatics and particularly his theory of the constitution of empirical concepts (as published in *Der logische Aufbau der Welt*) proved a very stimulating source of discussions. In the same year also, Ludwig Wittgenstein's *Tractatus Logico-Philosophicus* was studied by the Circle. The philosophical position of Logical Positivism in its original form was the outcome of these profoundly incisive influences. Though many of the basic ideas had already been enunciated in a general manner by Schlick, they were formulated more precisely, stated more fully and radically, by Carnap and Wittgenstein, quite independently. These two men exerted an enormous influence upon Schlick, who was about ten years their senior.

"In contrast to Carnap, who became a regular and most influential participant in the group, Wittgenstein, then preoccupied with architecture, associated only occasionally with some of the members of the Circle. Even thus, more light was obtained on some of the rather obscurely written passages of his extremely condensed and profound *Tractatus*. A few years later Wittgenstein returned to his philosophical studies and was called to Cambridge, England, where he later became successor to G. E. Moore. Schlick, as a visiting Professor, went to California in 1929 and 1932. Carnap was called to Prague in 1930 (later, in 1936, to Chicago) and Feigl to the United States in 1930. Hans Hahn, who was an expert in *Principia Mathematica* and in general an enthusiastic follower of Russell, died prematurely in 1934. The Circle discussions, however, continued, with Schlick and Waismann leading, until Schlick's tragic death in 1936. A former student, for years under observation by psychiatrists and diagnosed as insane, assassinated Schlick. The passing of this kindly, truly great and noble man, was bitterly lamented by his many friends.

"The discussions of the Circle centered about the foundations of logic and mathematics, the logic of empirical knowledge, and only occasional excursions into the philosophy of the social sciences and ethics. Despite the many differences of opinion, there was a remarkable spirit of friendly cooperation in the Circle. The procedure was definitely that of a joint search for clarity."[2]

3. The Program

A more detailed exposition of the work of the Vienna Circle was given in 1929 in a publication entitled *Wissenschaftliche Weltauffassung: Der Wiener Kreis*, which marked the appearance of the Circle before the public as an organization with a scientific as well as an educational purpose. The publication was sent out by the Verein Ernst Mach, which was founded in November, 1928, with Schlick as a president, and had for its object to "further and propagate a scientific world view," as conceived by the members of the Circle, through public lectures and writings. According to this pamphlet, the main lines of their program may be described as follows:

The aim is to form an *Einheitswissenschaft*, i.e., a unified science comprising all knowedge of reality accessible to man without dividing it into separate, unconnected special disciplines, such as physics and psychology, natural science and letters, philosophy and the special sciences. The way to attain this is by the use of the *logical method of analysis*, worked out by Peano, Frege, Whitehead, and Russell, which serves to eliminate metaphysical problems and assertions as meaningless as well as to clarify the meaning of concepts and sentences of empirical science by showing their immediately observable content—"das Gegebene." In both respects the Vienna Circle continues the endeavors initiated by Ernst Mach; but, by the application of logical analysis, which is a distinctive feature of the new empiricism, and of positivism, as compared to the older forms of these movements, it obtains a hitherto unattained completeness and precision. The culmination so far has been reached in the "constitution theory" advanced by Rudolf Carnap in *Der logische Aufbau der Welt* (Berlin, 1928), according to which any tenable concept of real objects is constituted by being reduced to characteristics of that which is immediately given, and any meaningful statement is constituted by being reduced to a statement of the given. Thus a framework is created for the work of the Vienna Circle; its negative task is an expurgation of metaphysical-speculative statements as meaningless, while its positive task is to define ever more precisely and fully the meaning of scientifically tenable statements. "If anyone asserts: 'There is a God,' 'The first cause of the world is the Unconscious,' 'There is an entelechy which is the leading principle in living beings,' we do not say 'What you say is false'; rather, we ask him, 'What do you mean by your statements?' It then appears that there is a sharp division between two types of statements. One of the types includes statements as they are made in empirical science; their meaning can be determined by logical analysis, or, more precisely, by reduction to simple sentences about the empirically given. The other statements, including those mentioned above, show themselves to be completely meaningless, if we take them as the metaphysician intends them. Of course, we can frequently reinterpret them as empirical statements. They then, however, lose the emotional content which is the very thing which is essential to the metaphysician. The metaphysicians and theologians, misinterpreting their own sentences, believe that their sentences assert something, represent some state of affairs. Nevertheless, analysis shows that these sentences do not say anything, being instead only an expression of some emotional attitude. To express this may certainly be a significant task. However, the adequate means for its expression is art, for example, lyric poetry or music. If, instead of these, the linguistic dress of a theory is chosen, a danger arises: a theoretical content, which does not exist, is feigned. If a metaphysician or theologian wishes to retain the usual form in language, he should understand thoroughly and explain clearly that it is not representation but expression; not theory, information, or cognition, but rather poetry or myth. If a mystic asserts that he has experiences that transcend all concepts, he cannot be challenged. But he cannot speak about it, since speaking means grasping concepts and reducing to facts which can be incorporated into science."[3]

The view of the Vienna Circle as to how such incorporation should be undertaken is particularly evident in the above-mentioned theory of constitution, which will be more explicitly dealt with presently. First, however, it would be expedient to look at the development of the opinions and points of view forming the background of the Circle's conception of philosophy and knowledge generally.

4. Predecessors

The forerunners of logical empiricism are, in the opinion of the members of the movement themselves, all those philosophers and scientists who show a clear antimetaphysical or antispeculative, realistic or materialistic, critical or skeptical, tendency—as well as everyone who has contributed essentially to the development of their most important methodological instrument: symbolic logic. In antiquity the Sophists and the Epicureans are mentioned; in the Middle Ages the nominalists; and in modern times, Neurath[4] gives the following three lists of names, indicating the lines of development in England, France, and Germany that may be said to lead in the direction of logical empiricism: Bacon, Hobbes, Locke, Hume, Bentham, J. S. Mill, Spencer; Descartes, Bayle, D'Alembert, Saint-Simon, Comte, Poincaré; Leibniz, Bolzano, Mach. In their programs similar lines of development are noticed, only here the grouping has been made according to subject and not according to nationality:

1. Positivism and empiricism: Hume, the philosophers of the Enlightenment, Comte, Mill, Avenarius, Mach.

2. The basis, aims, and methods (hypotheses in physics, geometry, etc.) of the empirical sciences: Helmholtz, Riemann, Mach, Poincaré, Enriques, Duhem, Boltzmann, Einstein.

3. Logistics and its application to reality: Leibniz, Peano, Frege, Schröder, Russell, Whitehead, Wittgenstein.

4. Axiomatics: Pasch, Peano, Vailati, Pieri, Hilbert.

5. Eudaemonism and positivistic sociology: Epicurus, Hume, Bentham, Mill, Comte, Feuerbach, Marx, Spencer, Müller-Lyer, Popper-Lynkeus, Carl Menger (the economist).

The predecessors and teachers here mentioned were the ones especially studied and discussed by the Vienna Circle. Not until later did the Circle discover the American pragmatists, instrumentalists, and operationalists to whom they are closely related in several respects and with whom they have since co-operated, as well as with certain other affiliated groups. I shall return to this point in the following chapter, having mentioned here only the authors whose works have actually played an important part in the development of the views of the Circle. There are, however, three of these philosophers whose influence has been so significant that they must be more explicitly dealt with: Ernst Mach, Bertrand Russell, and Ludwig Wittgenstein.

5. The Positivism of Ernst Mach

Mach (1838–1916), who started his scientific career as a professor of mathematics and later of physics, in 1895 received a professorship in philosophy, especially the history and theory of the inductive sciences, at the University of Vienna. Owing to bad health, however, he had to retire in 1901; he was succeeded by the well-known physicist, L. Boltzmann From his youth Mach had been vividly interested in philosophical and epistemological questions as well as in the historical development of the natural sciences. This appears clearly from his main works, *Die Mechanik in ihrer Entwicklung, historisch-kritisch dargestellt* (1883) (English trans., *The Science of Mechanics* [Chicago, 1893]), *Die Analyse der Empfindungen und das Verhältnis des Physischen zum Psychischen* (1886) (English trans., *The Analysis of Sensations* [Chicago, 1914]), *Die Prinzipien der Wärmelehre, historisch-kritisch entwickelt* (1896), *Populär-wissenschaftliche Vorlesungen* (1896) (English trans., *Popular Scientific Lectures* [Chicago, 1895]), *Erkenntnis und Irrtum: Skizzen zur Psychologie der Forschung* (1905), and *Die Prinzipien der physikalischen Optik, historisch und erkenntnispsychologisch entwickelt* (finished 1913, published 1921) (English trans., *Principles of Physical Optics* [New York, 1926]).

In these books Mach advanced his positivistic theory of knowledge, according to which human knowledge from its most primitive forms to the heights of science is a biological phenomenon, part of the history of man. Influenced by Darwin's theory of evolution, he conceived knowledge as a never ending process of adjustment of thoughts to reality and to each other. A priori and eternal truths do not exist, nor is there any difference in principle between axioms and deduced sentences. All statements concerning the world, particular as well as general rules, natural laws, theories, and principles, are subject to continuous control and modification by experience. Even geometrical sentences are, in so far as they are statements about reality, empirical sentences whose validity depends simply on immemorial observations of regularities in the spatial conditions and movements of things; so considered, geometry is a part of natural science of the same kind as mechanics or the theory of heat or the theory of electricity. Accordingly, we are not bound to follow any definite kind of geometry but may choose the one that appears to attain most expediently the most thought-saving description of experiences of the spatial relations of things. Space itself is merely the totality of the spatial relations of things, and not—as believed by Newton and Kant—an empty container in which things have been located in "absolute" places or in which they perform "absolute" movements.

On a closer examination, things, too, appear to be merely relatively constant complexes of so-called "qualities," which Mach identified with our sensations and called "elements." A "thing-in-itself" existing behind these elements is a metaphysical illusion, presumably due to the fact that the same names are used to designate things, even though these change, so that we are led to believe that the "same" thing persists throughout the changes. What we do observe is actually never any such hidden things but simply qualities of their mutual relations. Natural laws should therefore be formulated as functional relations between the elements, i.e., between sensations such as green, hot, hard, extended, continuous, etc. These sensations are not in themselves illusory or deceptive, but, on the contrary, they are all that we know of reality. What we call "deception of the senses" is merely certain unusual complexes of elements deceiving us because they resemble familiar complexes and so raise expectations that are not fulfilled. If they are correctly conceived, there is nothing deceptive about them. The point is to distinguish between the various contexts in which any given element may occur. These contexts are all equally real; but, if they are confused with one another, contradictions arise which we attempt to avoid by declaring one of their terms illusory. To a person measuring the site for a house, the surface of the earth is a plane, but to the person undertaking an exact measurement of the total surface of the globe, it is a spheroid. There is no contradiction in this, if only it is realized that the observations are made under different conditions and in different ways and that the words describing them take on different meanings when we pass from one standpoint to another. 'Up' and 'down', for instance, are everyday terms which have an easily understood sense in the world of our everyday life but which lose this sense when we proceed to describe the universe astronomically. And similarly the words 'red', 'yellow', and 'blue' are names designating sensations, and as such are well suited to describe the phenomena of our daily life; however, they must be replaced by words like 'wave movements' or 'corpuscle rays' if we want to describe the more subtle phenomena and contexts of phenomena observed by the physicist in his investigations of color. One kind of observation is not truer or more faithful to reality than is the other, but the contexts in which they occur differ and must be described by different words. Every scientific statement is a statement about complexes of sensations, and beyond or behind these there are no realities to be looked for, because the word 'reality' itself is merely a name for the sum total of the complexes of observable sensations.

What has been said here of physical things, according to Mach, also applies to the so-called "mental substances" of egos: they are merely special complexes of elements, even complexes with fluctuating boundaries, now expanding and now narrowing, but continuously changing in the course of life, disappearing in a dreamless sleep and altering completely in case of a mental disease or other abnormality. Although of great practical importance in our daily life, the word 'ego' does not signify any unchangeable or eternal object of a specific "mental" character; indeed, the difference between physical and psychical phenomena does not depend on the nature of the phenomena but solely on the context in which they occur: if a sensation is conceived as a link in a physical natural law, it is called a "physical phenomenon" or a quality of a physical thing, but if it is conceived as a link in a psychological law–directed regularity, i.e., as dependent according to natural law upon the condition of the observer, it is called a "psychical phenomenon." Physical and psychical phenomena are not essentially different, and all statements concerning them are of exactly equal rank, since they can all be reduced to statements about complexes of sensations which are all that is given or immediately observable.

In this the positivism of Mach differs from that of Comte. In Comte—who created the word 'positivism'—'positive', 'supposed', or 'given' signifies, in the first place, observable physical objects as opposed to fictive, speculatively constructed metaphysical entities; and in his system he found no room for psychology itself but classed it, without giving a detailed explanation, under biology. Further, the system of sciences assumed in Comte a hierarchic character, the six basic sciences—mathematics, astronomy, physics, chemistry, biology, and sociology, each presupposing the preceding ones without being capable of being deduced from them; this, expressed differently, means that the "higher" phenomena cannot be reduced to the lower; accordingly, the idea of a unity of science is incompatible with Comte's conception of the hierarchy of the sciences, whereas this idea was anticipated by Mach in his theory that all scientific statements should be reduced to statements of sensations. In this respect Comte's positivism is nearer to the dialectical materialism of Marx and the modern theory of emergent evolution than is the positivism of Mach—a fact which finds expression in Lenin's keen criticism of "Machism" in his *Materialismus und Empiriokriticismus* (1909) (English trans., *Materialism and Empirio-Criticism*, in *Collected Works of Lenin*, Vol. XIII [New York, 1927]). Although logical empiricists reject this criticism as being partially due to misunderstanding and consider themselves in accord with materialism[5] in all essentials, it cannot be denied that the positivism of the Vienna Circle is more closely related to the English empiricists than to the French materialists, with whom, from an epistemological point of view, it has, strictly speaking, in common only a strong aversion to speculative thinking. Among its great teachers we do not find the French encyclopedists or Comte, but Bertrand Russell;[6] Russell, the greatest living representative of English empiricism, may not unjustly be called the "father" of logical positivism, since in him is found for the first time the conscious and extensive application of logical analysis to the problems of epistemological empiricism,[7] a position which was reached by neither Comte nor Mach but which is characteristic of logical empiricism.[8]

6. The Logical Positivism of Bertrand Russell

Bertrand Russell (born 1872) is one of the great pioneers of modern logistics. In his *The Principles of Mathematics* (1903) and in *Principia mathematica*, Volumes I–III (1910–13), which he wrote in collaboration with Alfred North Whitehead (1861–1947), Russell made a more critical and comprehensive attempt than had yet been made to develop a symbolic logic and to show that all pure mathematics may be reduced to formal logic. This reduction he attempted to carry through by (*a*) trying to define all the main concepts of mathematics (such as the concepts of natural numbers and of the various kinds of numbers, the basic concepts of the theory of manifolds, and concepts like continuity and derivative) by means of half-a-dozen basic logical concepts and (*b*) by trying to prove all the axioms of mathematics by means of half-a-dozen logical axioms. In other words, the arithmetization of mathematical analysis, already carried through to a large extent by various mathematicians, Russell attempted to carry on by logicizing all mathematics, the concept of a natural number being, for instance, defined as "a class of similar classes." It is true that the attempt was not altogether successful; but its disadvantages as well as its advantages, and the wealth of ideas it contained, made it a unique source of inspiration to logicians, to investigators of the foundations of mathematics, and to philosophers. From among its many new features we shall mention here only three which came to play a special part in the formation of logical positivism.

The study of logical paradoxes and of paradoxes within the theory of sets led Russell to set forth the theory of logical types, according to which, for instance, every class is of a higher type than are its members and every statement about another statement is of a higher type than the one about which it is made. If the types are kept apart, paradoxes can be avoided, whereas there is a risk of such paradoxes if the types are confused. Russell maintained that statements containing confusions of types are meaningless, even if, according to the usual linguistic syntax, they are correctly constructed; and so he replaced the current logical division of statements into true and false by the tripartition: true, false, and meaningless.

Another important partition of statements introduced in connection with the theory of types was the division into (1) elementary statements, i.e., statements whose truth or falsity may be realized without any knowledge of individual objects or qualities or relations other than the ones whose names occur in the statement in question, and (2) generalized statements, i.e., statements presupposing classes of individuals, qualities, or relations (which must be divided into a hierarchy of ascending types). The elementary statements are subdivided into (*a*) atomic statements, i.e., statements containing no other statements as constituents, and (*b*) molecular statements, i.e., statements containing other statements as constituents. An especially important group of the latter are the so-called "truth-functions," i.e., molecular statements, the truth or falsity of which does not depend upon the meaning of the statements forming part of them but solely upon their truth-values, i.e., their truth or falsity, such as, for instance, negations, disjunctions, conjunctions, conditionals, and biconditionals of elementary statements.

Further, Russell and Whitehead introduced the so-called "principle of abstraction," that may equally well be called "the principle which dispenses with abstraction": "When a group of objects have that kind of similarity which we are inclined to attribute to possession of a common quality, the principle in question shows that membership of the group will serve all the purposes of the supposed common quality, and that therefore, unless some common quality is actually known, the group or class of similar objects may be used to replace the common quality which need not be assumed to exist."[9] Any statement of the common quality may be replaced by a statement saying that something is a member of the class. 'Red', for instance, may be defined by our pointing at a red object and saying that everything of the same color as that object is red, making it unnecessary to analyze this quality further; and, similarly, the cardinal number three may be defined as the class of all classes having the same number of members as, for instance, the class of Paris, London, and Berlin, making it unnecessary to assume that all these triads possess a common quality.

In *Principia mathematica* formal logic was generalized, systematized, and made precise to such an extent, and couched in such expedient symbolic language, that we understand the great expectations of Russell when he said: "The old logic put thought in fetters, while the new logic gives it wings. It has, in my opinion, introduced the same kind of advance into philosophy as Galileo introduced into physics, making it possible at last to see what kinds of problems may be capable of solution, and what kinds must be abandoned as beyond human powers. And where a solution appears possible, the new logic provides a method which enables us to obtain results that do not merely embody personal idiosyncrasies, but must command the assent of all who are competent to form an opinion."[10]

This statement is found in the lectures on our knowledge of the external world which Russell delivered in Boston in 1914 and in which for the first time he used his new logical-analytical method for the solution of epistemological problems. The leading principle was here a form of Occam's razor or law of parsimony: "Entia non sunt multiplicanda praeter necessitatem." Russell later stated this principle in this form: "Wherever possible, substitute constructions out of known entities for inferences to unknown entities";[11] in the lectures here referred to he formulates it in the following way: "In other words, in dealing with any subject-matter, find out what entities are undeniably involved, and state everything in terms of these entities. Very often the resulting statement is more complicated and difficult than one which, like common sense and most philosophy, assumes hypothetical entities whose existence there is no good reason to believe in. We find it easier to imagine a wall-paper with changing colours than to think merely of the series of colours, but it is a mistake to suppose that what is easy and natural in thought is what is most free from unwarrantable assumptions, as the case of 'things' very aptly illustrates."[12]

The example to which he here refers is the analysis of things given in his lectures. Briefly expressed, it says that what we call a "thing" is not a permanent substance different from its changing qualities or appearances but may be defined as "a certain series of appearances, connected with each other by continuity and by certain causal laws."[13] To this view he was led by the following reasoning: every philosophical investigation starts from certain data which we must assume as being, on the whole and in a certain sense, pragmatically true. The data resisting the influence of critical reflection Russell calls "hard data" and thinks they are of two sorts: "the particular facts of sense, and the general truths of logic,"[14] to which must be added certain facts of memory and some introspective facts. By "facts of sense" he means "facts of *our own* sense-data" and maintains that *"in so far* as physics or common sense is verifiable, it must be capable of interpretation in terms of actual sense-data alone. The reason for this is simple. Verification consists always in the occurrence of an expected sense-datum. . . . Now if an expected sense-datum constitutes a verification, what was asserted must have been about sense-data; or, at any rate, if part of what was asserted was not about sense-data, then only the other part has been verified."[15] In order to be verifiable, statements of the external world must accordingly be about our own sense-data. Or, in other words, verifiable statements of the external world must be capable of definition or construction in terms of our own sense-data.

"For instance, a thing may be defined as 'a certain series of appearances, connected with each other by continuity and by certain causal laws.' In the case of slowly changing things, this is easily seen. Consider, say, a wall-paper which fades in the course of years. It is an effort not to conceive of it as one thing whose colour is slightly different at one time from what it is at another. But what do we really *know* about it? We know that under suitable circumstances—i.e. when we are, as is said, 'in the room'—we perceive certain colours in a certain pattern: not always precisely the same colours, but sufficiently similar to feel familiar. If we can state the laws according to which the colour varies, we can state all that is empirically verifiable; the assumption that there is a constant entity, the wall-paper, which has these various colours at various times, is a piece of gratuitous metaphysics. We may, if we like, *define* the wall-paper as the series of its aspects. These are collected together by the same motives which led us to regard the wall-paper as one thing, namely a combination of sensible continuity and causal connection. More generally, a thing will be defined as a certain series of aspects, namely those which would commonly be said to be *of* the thing. To say that a certain aspect is an aspect *of* a certain thing will merely mean that it is one of those which, taken serially, *are* the thing. Everything will then proceed as before: whatever was verifiable is unchanged, but our language is so interpreted as to avoid an unnecessary metaphysical assumption of permanence."[16]

As will be seen, this theory is in accordance with that of Mach, only a little more cautiously and precisely expressed; just as natural numbers are analyzed or constructed or defined as classes of classes, so the things of the external world are analyzed, constructed, or defined as combinations of sense-data. Similar conditions apply to various other entities which Russell defines in terms of sense-data alone, so that statements about them are reduced to statements about sense-data; later on he extended and modified these analyses in his *Analysis of Mind* (1921), in *The Analysis of Matter* (1927), as well as in *An Outline of Philosophy* (1927), without, however, changing his basic views in principle.

In a similar way, Whitehead analyzed in *The Organization of*

Thought (1917), in *An Enquiry concerning the Principles of Natural Knowledge* (1919), and in *The Concept of Nature* (1920), various physical concepts, the only difference being that he did not reduce them to sense-data but to so-called "events." Altogether, philosophical analysis of objects and statements became a main preoccupation of the Cambridge analysts. As a leader of this group along with Russell, and perhaps before him, G. E. Moore (born 1873) should be mentioned. Moore is the author of the modern analytical method which he endeavored to formulate with increasing precision and subtlety without, however, drawing any positivistic conclusions from it; in the Preface to his *Principia ethica* (1903) he clearly indicated his method in the following words: "It appears to me that in ethics, as in all other philosophical studies, the difficulties and disagreements, of which its history is full, are mainly due to a very simple cause: namely, to the attempt to answer questions without first discovering precisely *what* question it is which you desire to answer. I do not know how far this source of error would be done away with if philosophers would *try* to discover what question they were asking before they set about to answer it; for the work of analysis and distinction is often very difficult: we may often fail to make the necessary discovery, even though we make a definite attempt to do so. But I am inclined to think that in many cases a resolute attempt would be sufficient to ensure success; so that, if only this attempt were made, many of the most glaring difficulties and disagreements in philosophy would disappear. At all events, philosophers seem, in general, not to make the attempt; and, whether in consequence of this omission or not, they are constantly endeavouring to prove that 'Yes' or 'No' will answer questions, to which *neither* answer is correct, owing to the fact that what they have before their minds is not one question, but several, to some of which the true answer is 'No,' to others 'Yes.' "[17] Through his penetrating endeavors to apply the method of analysis outlined above, Moore demonstrated convincingly the extreme difficulty of stating *exactly* the sense of many everyday assumptions and expressions, and his great carefulness and caution kept him from formulating far-reaching hypotheses or maintaining definite views. But his acute, painstaking endeavor itself exercised a profound influence on a large number of his pupils in England, among whom may be mentioned C. D. Broad, L. S. Stebbing, F. P. Ramsey, J. T. Wisdom, A. E. Duncan-Jones, A. J. Ayer, M. Black, H. B. Acton, R. B. Braithwaite, K. Britton, W. Kneale, H. Knight, M. MacDonald, C. A. Mace, A. M. MacIver, C. A. Paul, G. Ryle, J. W. Reeves, and, most important, Ludwig Wittgenstein, who attended Moore's lectures during the years 1912–14 and was later, from 1939 to 1948, his successor to the professorship at Cambridge.[18] As Wittgenstein has played a greater part than any other one philosopher in the development of the Vienna Circle, which seems not to have had any close knowledge of Moore, it will be necessary to deal a little more explicitly with his original philosophy.

7. Ludwig Wittgenstein's Logical-philosophical Treatise

The only published philosophical work by Wittgenstein, *Tractatus logico-philosophicus*, is in many respects a highly remarkable achievement. Appearing first in Oswald's *Annalen der Naturphilosophie* in 1921, it was published the following year in London as an independent book, containing the original German text together with an English translation, the latter being carefully revised by the author himself. Its contents are formulated as a series of aphorisms with comments. The comments contain specifications of the main propositions and more or less detailed justifications or illustrations of them. There is no proper deductive context, and often it may be difficult to see whether a proposition is put forward as a mere postulate or as the result of an unformulated argument. Consequently, the book is anything but easy to read, and to this day several parts of it are not completely understood. When, in spite of this, it has aroused such vital interest in expert circles, this is due to the fact that it contains, beyond doubt, remarkable discoveries and ideas of a logical and epistemological nature and that altogether it bears witness to a rare originality and acuteness. It is extremely regrettable that a commentary by Friedrich Waismann, announced for several years, has not been published. However, within the Vienna Circle, where Waismann and Schlick were periodically in touch with Wittgenstein, the book was thoroughly discussed; and through the publications of the Circle, as well as through Russell's Introduction to the English edition, certain of its fundamental new ideas gradually became more widely known. The most important of these, which may be considered largely as a critical development of Russell's thought, are contained in the main propositions of the book:

"1. The world is everything that is the case.

"2. What is the case, the fact, is the existence of atomic facts.

"3. The logical picture of the facts is the thought.

"4. The thought is the significant proposition.

"5. Propositions are truth-functions of elementary propositions. (An elementary proposition is a truth-function of itself.)

"6. The general form of truth-function is: $[\bar{p}, \xi, N(\xi)]$. This is the general form of proposition.

"7. Whereof one cannot speak, thereof one must be silent."

In order to understand these propositions, it is necessary to make clear what problem it is that Wittgenstein tries to solve in his treatise. To use the words of Russell, "What relation must one fact (such as a sentence) have to another in order to be *capable* of being a symbol for that other?"[19] To which Wittgenstein answers as follows:

The symbolizing fact must be a picture of what is symbolized, in the sense that it must be of the same form or structure as that which is symbolized. To every element in the one must correspond one and only one element in the other, and the elements of the two facts must be similarly arranged. They must be related to each other as a figure to its projection or as a gramophone record or the musical thought or the score or the waves of sound are related to one another, so that they can be deduced from each other mutually by means of a kind of "law of projection" (4.014; 4.0141). In the natural languages this relation of projection is highly imperfect, and that is just why our everyday language gives rise to many misunderstandings and senseless philosophical problems. "Most propositions and questions, that have been written about philosophical matters, are not false, but senseless. We cannot, therefore, answer questions of this kind at all, but only state their senselessness. Most questions and propositions of the philosophers result from the fact that we do not understand the logic of our language. (They are of the same kind as the question whether the Good is more or less identical than the Beautiful.) And so it is not to be wondered at that the deepest problems are really *no* problems" (4.003). "All philosophy is 'critique of language' (but not at all in Mauthner's sense). Russell's merit is to have shown that the apparent logical form of the proposition need not be its real form" (4.0031).

This basic thought and its consequences are further illustrated by the comments on the first six main propositions. As to No. 1, the comment simply says that the world consists of facts and that these are independent of one another. As to No. 2, it is observed that atomic facts are combinations of objects (entities, things) that are simple. The way in which objects hang together in an atomic fact is the form of the atomic fact. To the atomic facts correspond atomic propositions, the forms of which must be identical with those of the corresponding facts. "We make to ourselves pictures of facts" (2.1). "The picture is a model of reality" (2.12). "To the objects correspond in the picture the elements of the picture" (2.13). "The picture consists in the fact that its elements are combined with one another in a definite way" (2.14). "In order to be a picture a fact must have something in common with what it pictures" (2.16). "What the picture must have in common with reality in order to be able to represent it after its manner—rightly or falsely—is its form of representation" (2.17). "The picture, however, cannot represent its form of representation; it shows it forth" (2.172). "The picture has the logical form of representation in common with what it pictures" (2.2). "The picture agrees with reality or not; it is right or wrong, true or false" (2.21). "What the picture represents is its sense" (2.221). "In the agreement or disagreement of its sense with reality, its truth or falsity consists" (2.222). "In order to discover whether the picture is true or false we must compare it with reality" (2.223). "It cannot be discovered from the picture alone whether it is true or false" (2.224). "There is no picture which is apriori true" (2.225). A distinction must therefore be made between the truth of a picture and its sense: the sense is that which it represents, but whether it is true or false depends on whether it represents a fact or not, which cannot be decided a priori.

As to No. 3, Wittgenstein observes that "the totality of true thoughts is a picture of the world" (3.01) and that "in the proposition the thought is expressed perceptibly through the senses" (3.1). "In the proposition the name represents the object" (3.22), but "only the proposition has sense, only in the context of a proposition has a name a meaning" (3.3). "If we change a constituent part of a proposition into a variable, there is a class of propositions which are all the values of the resulting variable proposition. This class in general still depends on what, by arbitrary agreement, we mean by parts of that proposition. But if we change all those signs, whose meaning was arbitrarily determined, into variables, there always remains such a class. But this is now no longer dependent on any agreement; it depends only on the nature of the proposition. It corresponds to a logical form, to a logical prototype" (3.315). In order to avoid the errors due to the imperfection of our everyday language, we must employ a symbolism which excludes them, "a symbolism, that is to say, which obeys the rules of *logical* grammar—of logical syntax" (3.325). "In logical syntax the meaning of a sign ought never to play a rôle . . ." (3.33).

In the comments on No. 4 Wittgenstein develops his theory of the logical correspondence between propositions and reality. "The proposition is a picture of reality, for I know the state of affairs presented by it, if I understand the proposition. And I understand the proposition, without its sense having been explained to me" (4.021). "The proposition *shows* its sense. The proposition *shows* how things stand, *if* it is true. And it *says*, that they do so stand" (4.022). "To understand a proposition means to know what is the case, if it is true. (One can therefore understand it without knowing whether it is true or not.) One understands it if one understands its constituent parts" (4.024). "The meanings of the simple signs (the words) must be explained to us, if we are to understand them. By means of propositions we explain ourselves" (4.026). "One name stands for one thing, and another for another thing, and they are connected together. And so the whole, like a living picture, presents the atomic fact" (4.0311). "The possibility of propositions is based upon the principle of the representation of objects by signs. My fundamental thought is that the 'logical constants' do not represent. That the *logic* of the facts cannot be represented" (4.0312). "In the proposition there must be exactly as many things distinguishable as there are in the state of affairs, which it represents. They must both possess the same logical (mathematical) multiplicity (cf. Hertz's *Mechanics*, on Dynamic Models)" (4.04). "This mathematical multiplicity naturally cannot in its turn be represented. One cannot get outside it in the representation" (4.041). "Reality is compared with the propositions" (4.05). "Propositions can be true or false only by being pictures of the reality" (4.06). "Every proposition must *already* have a sense: assertion cannot give it a sense, for what it asserts is the sense itself. And the same holds of denial, etc." (4.064). "A proposition presents the existence and non-existence of atomic facts" (4.1). "The totality of true propositions is the total natural science (or the totality of the natural sciences)" (4.11). "Philosophy is not one of the natural sciences. (The word 'philosophy' must mean something which stands above or below, but not beside, the natural sciences.)" (4.111). "The object of philosophy is the logical clarification of thoughts. Philosophy is not a theory but an activity. A philosophical work consists essentially of elucidations. The result of philosophy is not a number of 'philosophical propositions,' but to make propositions clear. Philosophy should make clear and delimit sharply the thoughts which otherwise are, as it were, opaque and blurred" (4.112). "Propositions can represent the whole reality, but they cannot represent what they must have in common with reality in order to be able to represent it—the logical form. To be able to represent the logical form, we should have to be able to put ourselves with the propositions outside logic, that is, outside the world" (4.12). ". . . That which expresses *itself* in language, *we* cannot express by language. The propositions *show* the logical form of reality . . ." (4.121). "What *can* be shown *cannot* be said" (4. 1212).

These more or less obscure assertions were eagerly discussed within the Vienna Circle, and, as will appear from what follows, they have on essential points determined the view of the Circle on philosophy and its relation to the special sciences. However, for the time being, I will let this matter rest and pass to a short account of Wittgenstein's important theory of the truth-functions which is stated in the remaining part of the comments on No. 4 and in the comments on No. 5. He says here:

"The sense of a proposition is its agreement and disagreement with the possibilities of the existence and non-existence of the atomic facts" (4.2). "The simplest proposition, the elementary proposition, asserts the existence of an atomic fact" (4.21). "It is a sign of an elementary proposition, that no elementary proposition can contradict it" (4.211). "The elementary proposition consists of names. It is a connexion, a concatenation, of names" (4.22). "It is obvious that in the analysis of propositions we must come to elementary propositions, which consist of names in immediate combination . . ." (4.221). "If the elementary proposition is true, the atomic fact exists; if it is false the atomic fact does not exist" (4.25). "The specification of all true elementary propositions describes the world completely. The world is completely described by the specification of all elementary propositions plus the specification, which of them are true and which false" (4.26). "The truth-possibilities of the elementary propositions mean the possibilities of the existence and non-existence of the atomic facts" (4.3).

If the truth-values (truth or falsehood) of the elementary propositions are combined in every possible way, a survey is obtained of the total number of truth-possibilities, which corresponds to a survey of the total number of possible combinations of all atomic facts. To every combination of atomic facts corresponds a combined molecular proposition, expressing which combinations of atomic facts exist and which do not exist, i.e., which combinations of truth-values of the corresponding atomic propositions exist and which do not exist. This may be presented by a truth-table which corresponds to a molecular proposition and may appear as follows:

p	q	
T	T	T
F	T	T
T	F	F
F	F	T

or shorter: $(TTFT)(p, q)$,

where 'p' and 'q' represent elementary propositions, and the 'T' and 'F' under each represent its possible truth-values, while the last column indicates whether the combinations of truth-values concerned exist or do not exist. Among the possible groups of molecular propositions, there are two extreme cases: the so-called "tautology," which is true for all truth-possibilities, and the so-called "contradiction," which is false for all truth-possibilities. They are without sense, but not senseless. "Tautology and contradiction are not pictures of the reality. They present no possible state of affairs. For the one allows *every* possible state of affairs, the other *none* . . ." (4.462).

According to No. 5, every proposition is now a truth-function of the elementary propositions, which are the truth-arguments of the proposition. In his comments Wittgenstein develops his theory of probability, his theory of the logical relation of inference, and his theory that all logical propositions are tautologies and therefore say nothing of the reality. Further, he criticizes Russell's theory of the relation of identity and develops his theory that it is possible to construct any truth-function from the elementary propositions by the successive application of single logical operations. "Every truth-function is a result of the successive application of the operation (- - - T) (ξ, . . .) to elementary propositions. This operation denies all the propositions in the right-hand bracket and I call it the negation of these propositions" (5.5). This development I shall now explain a little further.

As early as 1913 the American mathematician and logician, H. M. Sheffer,[20] showed that all the truth-functions used in *Principia mathematica* may be defined solely by means of the so-called "stroke-operation," which is written '$p|q$' and may be interpreted as 'not-p and not-q'. For instance, the negation of p and the disjunction of p and q may be defined as follows: $\sim p =_{Df} p|p$ and $p \vee q =_{Df} [(p|q)|(p|q)]$. Since the total number of other truth-functions of p and q may be defined by means of $\sim p$ and $p \vee q$, they may also be defined by repeated application of the stroke-operation. Wittgenstein's theory is a generalization of this from truth-functions with only one or two arguments to truth-functions with an arbitrary number of arguments. The principle is as follows:

If there is given only one elementary proposition, p, it is possible by means of the stroke-operation to construct: $p|p [=_{Df} \sim p], (p|p)|p [=_{Df} p \cdot \sim p], p|(p|p) [=_{Df} \sim p \cdot p], (p|p)|(p|p) [=_{Df} p \cdot p], \ldots$

If two and only two elementary propositions, p and q, are given, it is further possible to construct: $q|q [=_{Df} \sim q], (q|q)|q [=_{Df} q \cdot \sim q], \ldots p|q [=_{Df} \sim p \cdot \sim q], (p|q)|(p|q) [=_{Df} p \vee q], (p|p)|(q|q) [=_{Df} p \cdot q], ((p|p)|q)|((p|p)|q) [=_{Df} p \supset q], \ldots$

And it is possible to proceed in the same way no matter how many elementary propositions are given. Wittgenstein, writing instead of the above operation '$(- - - \text{T})(\xi, \ldots)$' its result '$N(\xi)$', i.e., the negation of the total number of variables of propositions ξ (5.502), expresses the method of construction in the general form of the truth-function $[\bar{p}, \xi, N(\xi)]$, where

'$\bar{p}$' stands for the class of all elementary propositions,
'ξ' stands for any class of propositions,
'$N(\xi)$' stands for the negation of all the propositions making up ξ.

The whole symbol '$[\bar{p}, \xi, N(\xi)]$' means whatever can be obtained by taking any selection of elementary propositions, negating them all, and then taking any selection of the class of propositions now obtained, together with any of the originals.[21] Or, in Wittgenstein's words: "This says nothing else than that every proposition is the result of successive applications of the operation $N'(\xi)$ to the elementary propositions" (6.001).

It is especially interesting that he also extends this method of construction to the so-called "generalized propositions," i.e., propositions of the form: "all x are f" (more exactly: "the propositional function fx is a true proposition for every value of x"), or of the form: "there are x's that are f" (more exactly: "the propositional function becomes a true proposition for at least one value of x"). In the current notation these propositions are written: '$(x) fx$' and '$(Ex) fx$', and Wittgenstein's theory is then expressed in the proposition: "If the values of ξ are the total values of a function fx for all the values of x, then $N(\xi) = \sim(Ex) fx$" (5.52). What this means, then, is that, by the application of the operation of negation $N'(\xi)$ to the class of propositions which are values of a given propositional function fx, one arrives at a proposition which says that it is false that there is at least one value of x for which fx is a true proposition. And by negation of this latter proposition one obtains the generalized existential proposition '$(Ex) fx$', that is, "there is at least one x, for which fx is a true proposition." Similarly, by starting from the negation of fx, not-fx, instead of from fx, it is possible to construct the generalized proposition '$(x) fx$', i.e., "fx is a true proposition for every value of x."

The remaining comments on No. 6 contain Wittgenstein's definition of natural numbers as exponents of operations and his theory that the propositions of mathematics are equations "and therefore pseudo-propositions" (6.2). It is impossible here to go into this question, but his view of logic must be briefly dealt with. He says:

"The propositions of logic are tautologies" (6.1). "The propositions of logic therefore say nothing. (They are the analytical propositions)" (6.11). "It is the characteristic mark of logical propositions that one can perceive in the symbol alone that they are true; and this fact contains in itself the whole philosophy of logic. And so also it is one of the most important facts that the truth or falsehood of non-logical propositions can *not* be recognized from the propositions alone" (6.113). "The fact that the propositions of logic are tautologies *shows* the formal—logical—properties of language, of the world . . ." (6.12). "The logical propositions describe the scaffolding of the world, or rather they present it. They 'treat' of nothing. They presuppose that names have meaning, and that elementary propositions have sense. And this is their connexion with the world. It is clear that it must show something about the world that certain combinations of symbols—which essentially have a definite character—are tautologies. Herein lies the decisive point. We said that in the symbols which we use much is arbitrary, much not. In logic only this expresses: but this means that in logic it is not *we* who express, by means of signs, what we want, but in logic the nature of the essentially necessary signs itself asserts. That is to say, if we know the logical syntax of any sign language, then all the propositions of logic are already given" (6.124). "Whether a proposition belongs to logic can be determined by determining the logical properties of the *symbol*. And this we do when we prove a logical proposition. For without troubling ourselves about a sense and a meaning, we form the logical propositions out of others by mere *symbolic rules*. We prove a logical proposition by creating it out of other logical propositions by applying in succession certain operations, which again generate tautologies out of the first. (And from a tautology only tautologies *follow*.) Naturally this way of showing that its propositions are tautologies is quite unessential to logic. Because the propositions, from which the proof starts, must show without proof that they are tautologies" (6.126). "Proof in logic is only a mechanical expedient to facilitate the recognition of tautology, where it is complicated" (6.1262). "All propositions of logic are of equal rank; there are not some which are essentially primitive and others deduced from these. Every tautology itself shows that it is a tautology" (6.127).

The remaining part of the comments on No. 6 are of a more sporadic character and are often merely short aphoristic remarks on various philosophical questions. I quote only the more important ones, which have exercised a certain influence on the philosophy of the Vienna Circle.

"Logical research means the investigation of *all regularity*. And outside logic all is accident" (6.3). "The law of causality is not a law but the form of a law" (6.32). "If there were a law of causality, it might run: 'There are natural laws . . .' " (6.36). "A necessity for one thing to happen because another has happened does not exist. There is only *logical* necessity" (6.37). "As there is only a *logical* necessity, so there is only a *logical* impossibility" (6.375). "It is clear that ethics cannot be expressed . . ." (6.421). "Death is not an event of life. Death is not lived through. . . . Our life is endless in the way that our visual field is without limit" (6.4311). "Not *how* the world is, is the mystical, but *that* it is" (6.44). "For an answer which cannot be expressed the question too cannot be expressed. *The riddle* does not exist. If a question can be put at all, then it *can* also be answered" (6.5). "The solution of the problem of life is seen in the vanishing of this problem . . ." (6.521). "There is indeed the inexpressible. This *shows* itself; it is the mystical" (6.522). "The right method of philosophy would be this: To say nothing except what can be said, i.e., the propositions of natural science, i.e., something that has nothing to do with philosophy: and then always, when someone else wished to say something metaphysical, to demonstrate to him that he had given no meaning to certain signs in his propositions. This method would be unsatisfying to the other—he would not have the feeling that we were teaching him philosophy—but it would be the only strictly correct method" (6.53). "My propositions are elucidatory in this way: he who understands me finally recognizes them as senseless, when he has climbed through them, on them, over them. (He must so to speak throw away the ladder, after he has climbed up on it.) He must surmount these propositions; then he sees the world rightly" (6.54).

And then the book concludes with No. 7 without comments: "Whereof one cannot speak, thereof one must be silent" (7).

The fascinating effect of this book on the members of the Vienna Circle will be understood, when it is kept in mind that it contained a series of important logical discoveries as well as a wealth of new philosophical views, the grounds for and consequences of which were often barely indicated and so left to be worked out in full by its readers. And, simultaneously, it contained an element of irritation because of its strange mixture of lucid clearness and obscure profundity. Logic and mysticism, elucidation and obscuration, were here found side by side and deeply impressed the members of the Circle and in particular Moritz Schlick, whose thoughts had already in several respects taken a similar trend. The book was eagerly discussed at the meetings of the Circle and contributed essentially to the formation of logical positivism and provoked both agreement and disagreement. In connection with the other influences formerly mentioned (see pp. 2–3), it led, in the course of the twenties, to the crystallization of the philosophical view characteristic of the Vienna Circle, to which Wittgenstein himself did not belong.

8. Rudolf Carnap's Theory of The Constitution of Concepts

Another influence of considerable importance in the formation of the views of the Circle was Carnap's "theory of constitution," put forward in his *Der logische Aufbau der Welt* ("The Logical Construction of the World") (1928), the main lines of which I shall now state briefly. Carnap (born 1891), who in 1926 became lecturer in Vienna and, later, professor in Prague and, since 1936, has been a professor in Chicago, had earlier published several contributions to the philosophy of geometry and physics, among which may be mentioned *Der Raum: Ein Beitrag zur Wissenschaftslehre* (1922) and *Physikalische Begriffsbildung* (1926). In these he had shown himself to be an exceptionally stringent and lucid thinker, and he soon became one of the leading figures within the Vienna Circle. His great systematic gifts bore their first large fruit in the above-mentioned work, *Der logische Aufbau der Welt*, to which were added, as supplementary writings, some minor publications of the same year, namely, *Scheinprobleme in der Philosophie: Das Fremdpsychische und der Realismusstreit* (Berlin, 1928) and *Abriss der Logistik, mit besonderer Berücksichtigung der Relationstheorie und ihrer Anwendungen* (Vienna, 1928). In the first of these, certain applications of the theory of constitution propounded in the main work are explained and treated, and the latter contains a brief and clear account of the logistic method used in the formulation of theories.

The purpose of the theory of constitution will perhaps be best understood if viewed in the light of its philosophical applications and results. These results, which may be described as a continuation and clarification of certain ideas of Mach, Russell, and Wittgenstein, go to show, positively, that all the concepts of the natural and social sciences may be defined by means of so-called "elementary experiences," so that all statements of those sciences may be tested or checked by means of such elementary experiences and, negatively, that many traditional philosophical problems are merely pseudo-problems, since, being based on untestable assertions, they are, strictly speaking, senseless. More accurately, Carnap defines his criterion of meaning as follows:

"The meaning of a statement consists in its expressing a (thinkable, not necessarily also an actual) state of affairs. If an (alleged) statement expresses no (thinkable) state of affairs, it has no meaning and hence is only apparently an assertion. If a statement expresses a state of affairs, it is at all events meaningful, and it is true if this state of affairs exists, and false if it does not. One can know whether a statement is meaningful before one knows whether it is true or false.

"If a statement contains only concepts which are already known or recognized, it derives its meaning from these. On the other hand, if a statement contains a new concept or one whose legitimacy (scientific applicability) is in question, one must specify its meaning. In order to do this, it is necessary and sufficient to state the (only thinkable) experiential situations in which it would be called true (not: 'in which it is true'), and those in which it would be called false."[22]

In order to be factual, statements must be founded on an experience: nonfounded statements are empty or meaningless. This principle is acknowledged and practiced in all the natural and social sciences (natural science, psychology, cultural science). But this means that the objects of these sciences must be "constituted" in such a way that every statement about them can be written as, or "translated" into, a founded statement that is equivalent with, i.e., that has the same truth-value as, the original one. To show how this may be done is the aim of the theory of constitution.

To facilitate the understanding of Carnap's method, it may be expedient to recall a few of the logistic concepts used in the theory of constitution. There is, in the first place, the concept "propositional function," by which is understood an expression that contains one or more variables and which, by substitution of suitable arguments for these, becomes a true or a false proposition. Propositional functions with only one variable may be called properties, and their extension is then constituted by the objects satisfying them, that is to say, the names of which, when inserted instead of the variable, make the propositional function a true proposition. The totality of these objects is also called the class of objects defined by the propositional function. If two or more propositional functions are satisfied by exactly the same arguments, they are said to be of the same extension or to be coextensive; and, by the introduction of a special "sign of extension" for a group of coextensive propositional functions, it is possible to formulate propositions of the whole group without regarding the conceptual content ('red', for instance) contained in the propositional functions, but retaining the truth-values of the propositions resulting from the functions. Although not objects, the extensions are often spoken of as if they were, and Carnap therefore uses the designation "quasi-objects" as a convenient manner of speaking.

By means of these concepts Carnap is able to formulate his theory of constitution as follows: To constitute an object means to reduce it to other objects, i.e., to formulate a general rule (a "rule of constitution" or a "constitutional definition") indicating the way in which a statement containing the name of the first object may be replaced by an equivalent statement not containing it.[23] In simple cases this consists of a rule to the effect that, whenever the name of the first object appears, a certain expression containing the names of other objects but not that of the first object be substituted for it (explicit definition).[24] If an explicit definition in this sense is not possible, a contextual definition may be used, i.e., a rule of transformation stating generally how statements in which the expression which is not explicitly definable occurs may be replaced by other statements where it does not occur. Both explicit and contextual definitions may thus be used for the elimination of certain expressions, whether these are explicitly definable or not.

As, according to the definition just given, constitutional definitions concern only extensions, the formulation of constitutional definitions may be designated as an extensional method of definition. "It depends on the 'thesis of extensionality.' In every statement about a concept, the concept should be interpreted extensionally, i.e., it should be represented by its extension (class, relation); or, more precisely, in every statement about a propositional function, the propositional function may be replaced by its sign of extension."[25]

It is now the task of the theory of constitution to arrange the objects of every science according to their reducibility. The system forms, as it were, a genealogy of objects, the roots of which are the objects which cannot be reduced to others, and the trunk and branches show to which other objects any given object may be reduced. What Russell and Whitehead did in *Principia mathematica* with regard to mathematics (reduced all mathematical concepts to the logical fundamental concepts) Carnap in his theory of constitution attempts to do with regard to the natural and social sciences, although, as far as the greater part is concerned, only in outlines and with a limited application of symbolic logic.

As the various sciences do not generally avail themselves of the logistic language in which Carnap's definitions are formulated, but use a more everyday realistic language, he is obliged to replace his logistic criterion on the reducibility of objects by the following criterion of reducibility in realistic formulation: "We call an object *a* 'reducible to objects *b, c* . . .' if for the existence of every state of affairs with regard to *a, b, c* . . . a *necessary and sufficient condition* may be given which depends only on objects *b, c.* . . ."[26] By means of this criterion he is able to find out whether a given object is capable of being reduced to another object or not, and he can thus ascertain the order in which the objects must be constituted to form a connected and all-inclusive system of constitution. As this order is not uniquely determined on every point, however, by the said criterion of reducibility, Carnap also uses epistemological priority as a principle of arrangement; and this he defines as follows: "One object (or type of object) is called epistemologically prior with respect to another if the second is known by means of the first and, therefore, knowing the first object is a precondition to the knowing of the second object."[27] In consequence of the latter principle of arrangement, Carnap may also conceive of his whole system of constitution as a "rational reconstruction of the formation of reality, a formation which in the actual process of cognition is made intuitively."[28]

Being of the opinion that the four main kinds of objects are cultural (*geistige*) objects, other minds (*fremdpsychische*), physical objects, and data of our own minds (*eigenpsychische*), Carnap finds that between these objects reducibility is possible in the order mentioned,[29] so that cultural objects may be reduced to other minds, these may be reduced to physical objects, and these again to the data of one's own mind. Briefly, his course of reasoning is as follows: cultural objects (i.e., historical, sociological objects, such as religion, ways and customs, state, etc.) are known partly through their "mental manifestations" (human ideas, feelings and acts of volition), partly through their "documentations" (i.e., physical products, such as things, documents, and the like), and may therefore be constituted on the basis of these. And the objects of other minds are known partly—and mainly—through expressions of emotions and thought, partly—although, so far, very imperfectly—through the brain processes corresponding to the mental phenomena, and may therefore be constituted on the basis of physical objects. And the latter, finally, are known by observation, i.e., by data of our own minds, on the basis of which they may therefore be constituted.[30]

It should continuously be kept in mind, however, that the independence of the various kinds of objects is by no means eliminated by constitution. The higher objects are not composed of the lower but belong to quite different types of objects, which is shown by the fact that they cannot meaningfully be substituted for one another in given statements.[31] The constitution merely shows that statements of higher objects may be translated into statements of lower objects without their truth-value being altered and that statements of any kind of objects may accordingly be tested by means of statements of the lowest kind, the data of our own minds. Likewise, it should be emphasized that the order of arrangement here chosen is not the only possible one. It is, as already mentioned, based on epistemological priority. But if for other reasons it is found expedient, one may very well use the physical objects (i.e., the material things of our everyday life) as the basic element, since in principle the objects of our own mind may be constituted from the brain processes by means of the psychophysical relation. In view of the knowledge of the various kinds of objects and their mutual relations which actually exist in the sciences, Carnap chooses the data of our own minds as a basis for his system of constitution, and he describes them in the following way:

"The egocentric basis we shall also call the *'solipsistic' basis*. This does not mean that solipsism itself is here presupposed in the sense of regarding only one subject and his experiences as the sole reality, consequently denying the reality of other subjects. The distinction between real and unreal objects is not made at the beginning of the system of constitution. At the beginning there is no distinction made between those experiences which are, on the basis of later constitution, distinguished as perception, hallucination, dream, etc. This distinction as well as the consequent distinction between real and unreal objects occurs only at a rather high level of constitution. . . . The basic region can also be called 'the given'; it must be noted, however, that there is no intention to presuppose something or somebody to whom the given is given. . . .[32] The given is without a subject."[33]

Having chosen the data of the "own mind" as basis, Carnap determines the so-called "elementary" experiences as basic elements within this sphere and by elementary experiences he understands "experiences in their totality and closed unity."[34]

The function of elementary experiences within the system is similar to that of sensations within Mach's system, but they differ from the latter in not being the results of an analysis, but concrete, complicated units of experience. As such, they cannot be divided up but only be submitted to a so-called "quasi-analysis" on the basis of similarities and other relations holding among them.[35] As the basic relation Carnap uses the recollection of similarity, by which he understands the relation subsisting between two elementary experiences, when a comparison between a recollection of the first elementary experience and the second elementary experience shows that there is an approximate or complete agreement between a certain quality in the one and a certain quality in the other.[36] And from this fundamental relation between the elementary experiences the various objects and kinds of objects are constituted as outlined below.

It should be observed, to begin with, that in building up his system of constitution Carnap employs primarily the logistic symbolic language in the formulation of his constitutional definitions. To make them more easily understood, however, he writes them simultaneously in three other languages, viz., our everyday word-language, the realistic language which is the one current in the empirical sciences, and a fictitious constructive language containing the operational rules for the construction of the objects defined.[37] Although the logistic language is more exact, the following examples of Carnap's constitutional definitions will be given in the realistic language, which does not require so much specific knowledge in order to be understood and which seems sufficient to give an impression of the character of the system.

First, 'elementary experiences' are defined as the members of the relation "recollection of similarity," and next 'part-similarity' is defined as the relation subsisting between two elementary experiences, either of which contains a constituent part similar to a constituent part of the other one. Then 'a region of similarity' is defined as the greatest possible class of qualities between which a part-similarity exists, and 'a quality-class' as the quasi-object that represents something common to elementary experiences; further, he defines 'sense-classes' as classes of abstractions of chains of similarity of qualities, i.e., as what is common for a series of qualities passing evenly into one another. The sense of sight is thereupon defined as a sense-class having the dimensional number five (namely, color tone, saturation, lightness, height, and width). Then he defines 'sensation', 'place of field of vision', 'being in the same place', and 'neighborhood', as well as 'equicolored', 'color class', 'neighboring colors', and 'preceding in time'. And this concludes Carnap's treatment of the lowest stage, the data of the own mind in the system of constitution, from which he passes to the intermediate stages, beginning with physical objects.

By 'physical objects' he understands the material objects of our everyday life, which are characterized, in the first place, by filling a certain part of space at a certain point of time: "Place, shape, size, and position belong to the set of determinators of every physical thing. In addition, at least one sense-quality— e.g., color, weight, temperature—also belongs to this set of determinators."[38] Their constitution starts with the constitution of the space-time world, which is defined as the class of world-points to which are assigned colors (or other sense-qualities), i.e., the points in the n-dimensional space of real numbers in so far as they serve for the assignment of the qualities mentioned. For such assignments twelve rules are given, of which we shall mention here only Nos. 9 and 10, since they concern a controversial point in positivistic theories: "9. In so far as there is no reason to the contrary, it is presumed that a point of the external world that is seen once exists before and after it is seen; its positions form a continuous world line. 10. It is further presumed, in so far as there is no reason to the contrary, that such points of the external world have the same or similar color at other times as they had at the time they were seen."[39] The visual objects are defined as bundles of world-lines, the neighborhood relations of which remain much the same for a long period, and *my body* as a visual object with a series of special characteristics. With the help of these concepts, tactual-visual objects and the remaining senses and sense-qualities are defined, whereupon the whole domain of the own mind is determined as the sum total of elementary experiences thus arranged plus the unconscious objects constituted in analogy to the color points not seen at the present moment, so that these objects "consist of nothing but an appropriate rearrangement of immediately presented objects."[40]

The *world of perception* constituted in the whole space-time world by the attribution of sense-qualities to the individual world-points is completed by analogical attribution in a way that in a sense corresponds partly to a postulate of causality, partly to a postulate of substance. Between the world of perception and *the physical world* there is this difference: while the former is constituted by the attribution of sense-qualities to the world-points, the latter is constituted by the attribution of numbers, the physical quantities; this makes it possible to formulate laws mathematically and to achieve a unique noncontradictory intersubjectivation. Within the physical world *biological objects* may then be constituted, including especially *human beings* with their *expressive movements*, and they form the basis of the higher stage: other minds and cultural objects.

For the relation of expression is used the relation between certain observable physical processes in *my body* and a class of data frequently occurring at the same time in *my mind;* the mind of another person can then be constituted by the attribution of the latter class to similar processes in the body of another person. Accordingly, it is stated that "there are no other minds without bodies" and "the whole of the *experience of other people consists*, therefore, in nothing but *a reordering of my experiences and their constituent parts*."[41] Also the communications of other persons and the utterances of factual statements may be constituted on the basis of the signs generally applied to these processes. And thus the road is open for the constitution of *the world of the other person*, which, by comparison with my own world of observation, gives rise to the constitution of *the intersubjective world* that forms the proper domain of the objects of science—all of it, however, only as certain ramifications of "my" system of constitution, which does not mean, of course, that such ramifications exist only in my mind or in my body but merely that they may be constituted from objects in my own mind, i.e., that statements of them are capable of being transformed into statements of my own mind without any change in the truth-values of the statements. The same applies to the cultural objects constituted from their manifestations, i.e., from the mental processes in which they are actualized or make themselves known. Thus the object "state," for instance, may be constituted as follows: "A *state* is a system of relations among people characterized in such and such a way by its manifestations, viz., the mental behavior of these people and their dispositions for such behavior, especially the behavior dispositions of one individual as conditioned by the actions of other people."[42] As to *the values*, these may be constituted from an earlier point in the system of constitution, viz., from *experiences of value*, such as experiences of bad or good conscience, or duty, or responsibility, or aesthetic experiences, etc. "This does not mean that values are psychologized any more than the constitution of physical objects meant that these were psychologized. The system of constitution does not speak this realistic language, but is neutral with respect to the metaphysical components of realistic statements. However, it translates statements about the relation between value and value-feelings into the constitutional language in a way analogous to the way propositions concerning the relation between physical objects and perceptions are translated. . . ."[43] With this we close our outline of the system of constitution."[44]

What, now, is achieved by this system? That it has been carried through in detail only as far as the fundamental part is concerned Carnap himself emphasizes repeatedly and that, accordingly, its universal application may involve several changes; but, apart from that, the question arises: What would be achieved by carrying it through completely?

The answer is that, if carried through, the system would show *that* and *how* the totality of statements about objects forming the subject matter of the various sciences are capable of being transformed into statements about immediate experiences having the same truth-values as the original statements. In other words, it would show that all scientific statements are capable of being verified or falsified by means of immediate experiences. This is the positive side of the matter. Negatively, it would show that it is superfluous to assume or apply other sources or means of knowledge than logic and immediate experience. Indeed, Carnap goes so far as to say that the allegation of such other sources of knowledge leads merely to metaphysical assumptions which are meaningless, i.e., incapable of being tested by experience. Only statements consisting solely of logical constants and terms capable of being constituted on the basis of experience have a meaning in the strict sense of this word. Therefore, the theory of constitution may be used to purge science and philosophy of meaningless statements and pseudo-problems. In principle all meaningful questions can be answered—in the affirmative or the negative. There are no insoluble riddles; the apparent insolubility of certain problems is due to the fact that they are based on meaningless assumptions.

"It is sometimes said that the answers to many questions cannot be put into concepts, that they cannot be expressed. But in that event even the question itself cannot be expressed. In order to see this, we will investigate more precisely *what constitutes the answer to a question.* In a strictly logical sense, the posing of a question consists in the presentation of a proposition and the setting of the task of establishing as true either this proposition itself or its negation. A proposition can be given only by the presentation of its sign, the sentence, which is composed of words or other symbols. It frequently occurs, especially in philosophy, that a series of words is given which is considered a sentence but which, in fact, is not. A series of words is not a sentence if it contains a word that is without meaning or (and this is more frequently the case) when all the individual words have a meaning but these meanings do not fit into the context of the sentence. . . . If a real question is presented, what is the situation with respect to the possibility of answering it? In that case a proposition is given, expressed in conceptual signs connected in a formally permissible manner. Every legitimate concept of science has, in principle, its definite place in the system of constitution ('in principle,' i.e., if not at present, then in a possible future stage of scientific knowledge); otherwise, it cannot be recognized as legitimate. Since we are concerned here only with answerability *in principle*, we disregard the momentary condition of science and consider the stage in which the concepts which appear in the given proposition are incorporated into the system of constitution. On the basis of its constitutional definition, we substitute for the sign of each of the concepts in the given sentence the defining expression and make, step by step, the further substitutions of constitutional definitions. . . . The sentence given in the posing of the question is thus so transformed that it expresses a definite (and, indeed, a formal and extensional) state of affairs in respect to the basic relation. We assume in the theory of constitution that it is in principle determinable whether or not a specified basic relation holds between two elementary experiences. However, the state of affairs mentioned is composed of such particular relational propositions; and, further, the number of elements among which the basic relations hold, viz., elementary experiences, is finite. From this it follows that the existence or nonexistence of the state of affairs in question is in principle determinable in a finite number of steps and thus the *question posed is in principle answerable.*"[45]

On these cardinal points the members of the Vienna Circle were in 1928 fairly well agreed. The discussions continued, however, and a further examination of the problems gave rise to difficulties which not only made Carnap modify his standpoint considerably but also resulted in certain divergencies of opinion within the Circle.[46] But before these divergent tendencies had made themselves felt, the Circle had become so firmly established and so convinced that its methods and fundamental views were basically correct that, after 1930, it decided to get into touch with similar-minded groups and persons in other countries, and its development during the decade which followed showed an increasing international activity and growing response from many different quarters. This led to an extension of the external frame, and the very fact that the circle of the participants in the discussions was so widened resulted, necessarily, in a broadening of the basis of discussion, since the persons attracted by the general attitude and program of the movement had, in many respects, very different standpoints and opinions regarding the details of *logical empiricism*, as the movement now came to be called; its adherents wanted to emphasize that they did not consider themselves tied to positivistic views in the more narrow and dogmatic sense. In the following chapter this energetic and comprehensive development, intensive as well as extensive, will be dealt with.

II. Logical Empiricism: Its Expansion and Elaboration

1. Publications, Congresses, and International Connections

Logical positivism was first introduced to an international forum of philosophical experts at the Seventh International Congress of Philosophy held at Oxford in 1930. Here Schlick read a paper on "The Future of Philosophy," in which, with as much enthusiasm for, as confidence in, the new method of philosophy, he heralded a new era in the history of philosophy. ". . . It appears that by establishing the natural boundaries of philosophy we unexpectedly acquire a profound insight into its problems; we see them under a new aspect which provides us with the means of settling all so-called philosophical disputes in an absolutely final and ultimate manner. This seems to be a bold statement, and I realize how difficult it is to prove its truth and, moreover, to make anyone believe that the discovery of the true nature of philosophy, which is to bear such wonderful fruit, has already been achieved. Yet it is my firm conviction that this is really the case and that we are witnessing the beginning of a new era of philosophy, that its future will be very different from its past, which has been so full of pitiful failures, vain struggles, and futile disputes.''[1]

The new view of philosophy advocated was that of Wittgenstein, which Schlick expressed in two assertions, one negative and one positive: (1) philosophy is not a science and (2) it is the mental activity of clarification of ideas. Clarifying our thoughts means discovering or defining the real meaning of our propositions, which must be done before their truth can be established. This latter part is the task of the special sciences, with which philosophy cannot compete. All metaphysical attempts to do so have been vain and have only led to mutual conflicts between varying systems. And the reason for this is now understood: "Most of the so-called metaphysical propositions are no propositions at all, but meaningless combinations of words; and the rest are not 'metaphysical' at all, they are simply concealed scientific statements the truth or falsehood of which can be ascertained by the ordinary methods of experience and observation.[2]

"How will philosophy be studied and taught in the future?

"There will always be men who are especially fitted for analysing the ultimate meaning of scientific theories, but who may not be skillful in handling the methods by which their truth or falsehood is ascertained. These will be the men to study and to teach philosophizing, but of course they would have to *know* the theories just as well as the scientist who invents them. Otherwise they would not be able to take a single step, they would have no object on which to work. A philosopher, therefore, who knew nothing except philosophy would be like a knife without a blade and handle. Nowadays a professor of philosophy very often is a man who is not able to make anything clearer, that means he does not really philosophize at all, he just talks about philosophy or writes a book about it. This will be impossible in the future. The result of philosophizing will be that no more books will be written about philosophy, but that *all* books will be written in a philosophical manner.''[3]

Schlick's prophecies, however, caused no great stir among the other members of the congress, and, if someone had foretold the immensely rapid development and the response which the movement was to evoke in the course of the coming decade, he would no doubt have been met with a skeptical shake of the head. Nevertheless, the movement gained speed very rapidly during the next few years. This was particularly due to the publication, begun in 1930, of the periodical *Erkenntnis* (edited by Hans Reichenbach and Rudolf Carnap) and to the various series of writings, among which must be especially mentioned the series "Schriften zur wissenschaftlichen Weltauffassung" (edited by Philipp Frank and Moritz Schlick) and "Einheitswissenschaft" (edited by Otto Neurath, Rudolf Carnap, Philipp Frank, and Hans Hahn until the death of the latter in 1934; thereafter by Neurath, Carnap, and Joergen Joergensen and, from 1938, Charles Morris). In the first series the following ten books were published:

R. VON MISES, *Wahrscheinlichkeit, Statistik und Wahrheit* (1928); Eng. trans.: *Probability, Statistics, and Truth* (New York, 1939).

R. CARNAP, *Abriss der Logistik* (1929).

M. SCHLICK, *Fragen der Ethik* (1930); Eng. trans.: *Problems of Ethics* (New York, 1939).

O. NEURATH, *Empirische Soziologie* (1931).

P. FRANK, *Das Kausalgesetz und seine Grenzen* (1932).

O. KANT, *Zur Biologie der Ethik: Psychopathologische Untersuchungen über Schuldgefühl und moralische Idealbildung, zugleich ein Beitrag zum Wesen des neurotischen Menschen* (1932).

R. CARNAP, *Logische Syntax der Sprache* (1934); Eng. trans.: *Logical Syntax of Language* (London and New York, 1937).

K. POPPER, *Logik der Forschung: Zur Erkenntnistheorie der modernen Naturwissenschaft* (1935).

J. SCHÄCHTER, *Prolegomena zu einer kritischen Grammatik* (1935).

V. KRAFT, *Die Grundlagen einer wissenschaftlichen Wertlehre* (1937).

In the second series the following seven monographs appeared:

H. HAHN, *Logik, Mathematik und Naturerkennen* (1933).

O. NEURATH, *Einheitswissenschaft und Psychologie* (1933).

R. CARNAP, *Die Aufgabe der Wissenschaftslogik* (1934).

P. FRANK, *Das Ende der mechanistischen Physik* (1935).

O. NEURATH, *Was bedeutet rationale Wirtschaftsbetrachtung* (1935).

NEURATH, BRUNSWIK, HULL, MANNOURY, and WOODGER, *Zur Enzyklopädie der Einheitswissenschaft. Vorträge* (1938).

R. VON MISES, *Ernst Mach und die empiristische Wissenschaftsauffassung* (1939).

In 1938 this series was supplemented by the "Library of Unified Science Series," in which only two volumes have appeared:

R. VON MISES, *Kleines Lehrbuch des Positivismus: Einführung in die empiristische Wissenschaftsauffassung* (1939).

H. KELSEN, *Vergeltung und Kausalität* (1941); Eng. trans.: *Society and Nature* (Chicago, 1943).

In 1938 was begun also the publication of the large *International Encyclopedia of Unified Science* (University of Chicago Press) long planned by Otto Neurath; a number of monographs in this work had appeared when World War II seriously slowed down the development of the enterprise. The monographs published are as follows:

OTTO NEURATH, NIELS BOHR, JOHN DEWEY, BERTRAND RUSSELL, RUDOLF CARNAP, and CHARLES MORRIS, *Encyclopedia and Unified Science* (1938).

V. F. LENZEN, *Procedures of Empirical Science* (1938).

C. MORRIS, *Foundations of the Theory of Signs* (1938).

L. BLOOMFIELD, *Linguistic Aspects of Science* (1939).

R. CARNAP, *Foundations of Logic and Mathematics* (1939).

J. DEWEY, *Theory of Valuation* (1939).

E. NAGEL, *Principles of the Theory of Probability* (1939).

J. H. WOODGER, *The Technique of Theory Construction* (1939).

G. DE SANTILLANA and E. ZILSEL, *The Development of Rationalism and Empiricism* (1941).

O. NEURATH, *Foundations of the Social Sciences* (1944).

P. FRANK, *Foundations of Physics* (1946).

In addition, the followers of the movement, in various parts of the world, published in the course of the thirties a number of works of varying size, the most important of which will be mentioned below, and, at the initiative of Otto Neurath, the indefatigable organizer, co-operation was initiated between empiricist and logicist periodicals in various countries.

This extensive publishing activity contributed greatly to the development of the movement, as did also the arrangement of a number of international congresses that gave the members of the Vienna Circle an opportunity of stating and discussing their ideas with other philosophers and scientists feeling a need for international co-operation on the basis of empiricist-scientific fundamental views advocated by the movement. Detailed reports of all these congresses have been published in *Erkenntnis*, in the *Journal of Unified Science* (the periodical continuing *Erkenntnis*), and in a special report of the congress at Paris in 1935, *Actes du congrès international de philosophie scientifique, Sorbonne, Paris, 1935* (Paris, 1936).

The first two of these congresses (called "Tagungen") were kept within rather narrow limits and were attended by a relatively small number of participants from Austria, Czechoslovakia, and Germany. The first was held in Prague in 1929 and comprised, besides a number of papers (by Hahn, Neurath, and Frank) containing general information on the views of the Vienna Circle, a series of papers and discussions on causality and probability (Reichenbach, von Mises, Paul Hertz, Waismann, and Feigl) and on the foundations of mathematics and logic (Adolf Fraenkel and Carnap). The latter subject again formed the main subject at the second conference, held at Königsberg in 1930. Here Carnap lectured on the logicistic, Arend Heyting on the intuitionist, and Johann von Neumann on the formalist foundation of mathematics, while Otto Neugebauer read a paper on pre-Greek mathematics, Reichenbach one on the physical concept of truth, and Werner Heisenberg one on the principle of causality and quantum mechanics. Furthermore, there were at the two meetings vivid and stimulating discussions on the subjects and problems dealt with.

The next congress was held at Prague in 1934. It was called a preparatory meeting (the Paris congress was being planned for the following year under the name of the "Congrès international de philosophie scientifique"). Attended by people from various countries who later became more or less intimately connected with the movement and who met here for the first time, the preparatory meeting achieved a more international character than the preceding meetings had. Among the favorably interested participants were Lukasiewicz, Tarski, Ajdukiewicz, Janina Hosiasson, and Marja Kokoszynska, Poles; Ernest Nagel and Charles Morris, Americans; Louis Rougier, Frenchman; Eino Kaila, Finn; and Joergen Joergensen, Dane, all of whom read papers and took part in the discussions. The members of the group also took an active part in the Eighth International Congress of Philosophy held at Prague during the following days. Here Neurath read a paper on unified science, Schlick on the concept of wholeness, Carnap on the method of logical analysis, Reichenbach on the significance of the concept of probability for knowledge, and Joergensen on the logical foundations of science. These details are mentioned because they convey an impression of the kinds of problems with which the group was concerned.

This impression will become more complete if we consider the main subjects discussed the following year at the large congress at Paris: scientific philosophy and logical empiricism (Enriques, Reichenbach, Carnap, Morris, Neurath, Kotarbinski, Wiegner, Chwistek), unity of science (Frank, Du Nouy, Brunswik, Gibrat, Neurath, Hempel and Oppenheim, and Walther), language and pseudo-problems (Tarski, Kokoszynska, Massignon, Masson-Oursel, Richard, Chevalley, Padoa, Greenwood, Rougier, Matisse, Feigl, Vouillemin), induction and probability (Reichenbach, Schlick, Carnap, De Finetti, Zawirski, Hosiasson), logic and experience (Ajdukiewicz, Benjamin, Renaud, Petiau, Destouches, Métadier, Habermann, Chwistek, Braithwaite, Tranekjaer Rasmussen, Grelling), philosophy of mathematics (Gonseth, Lautman, Juvet, Bouligand, Destouches, Mania, Jaskowski, Raymond, Becker, Schrecker), logic (Tarski, Helmer, Sperantia, Lindenbaum, Bachmann, Padoa, Malfitano, Honnelaitre, Bollengier, Bergmann), and history of logic and scientific philosophy (Scholz, Jasinowski, Raymond, Bachmann, Padoa, Tegen, Hollitscher, Ayer, Zervos, Joergensen, Frank, Heinemann). At this congress also the above-mentioned *International Encyclopedia of Unified Science* was planned, at the initiative of Neurath, and a committee was set up for the drafting of a uniform international logical notation.

The following year, in 1936, the Second International Congress for the Unity of Science was held at Copenhagen and had the problem of causality as its main theme. This congress included a paper by Niels Bohr on causality and complementarity, while Frank spoke on philosophical interpretations and misinterpretations of the quantum theory, Lenzen on the interaction between subject and object in observation, J. B. S. Haldane on some principles of causal analysis in genetics, Rashevsky on physicomathematical methods in biological and social sciences, Rubin on our knowledge of other men, Neurath on sociological predictions, Somerville on logical empiricism and the problem of causality in social science, Hempel on a purely topological form of non-Aristotelian logic, and Popper on Carnap's logical syntax. During the congress, news was received of the assassination of Moritz Schlick, who had sent in a paper on the quantum theory and cognizability of nature.

The next year, in 1937, a Unity of Science Congress was held again in Paris in connection with the Ninth International Congress of Philosophy (Congrès Descartes). As, in the arrangement of its sections, this congress had shown itself particularly interested in the representatives of logical empiricism and had devoted a special section to the unity of science, the congress of the logical empiricists was confined to a conference on the problems of scientific co-operation, especially in connection with the *Encyclopedia* and the unification of logical symbolism. At the main congress (Congrès Descartes), Carnap spoke on the unity of science based on the unity of language; Neurath on prediction and terminology in physics, biology, and sociology; Reichenbach on the principal features of scientific philosophy; Frank on modern physics and the boundary between subject and object; Grelling on the influence of the antinomies in the development of logic in the twentieth century; Hempel on a system of generalized negations; Tarski on the deductive method; and Oppenheim on class concepts and order concepts. Several representatives of movements allied to logical empiricism took an active part. This was the last of the international congresses of philosophy before the outbreak of World War II.

But the movement of logical empiricism found time for two more congresses before the great catastrophe. The first was held in 1938 at Cambridge, England, and the second in 1939 at Harvard University, Cambridge, Massachusetts. The Cambridge congress of 1938 had for its main theme the language of science, and it included papers on language and misleading questions (L. S. Stebbing), relations between logical positivism and the Cambridge school of analysis (M. Black), the diverse definitions of probability (M. Fréchet), languages with expressions of infinite length (Helmer), mathematics as logical syntax and formalization of a physical theory (Strauss), the logical form of probability-statements (Hempel), the language of science (M. Fréchet), experience and convention in physical theory (Lenzen), autonomy of the language of physics (Rougier), the realistic interpretation of scientific sentences (Donald C. Williams), the formalization of a psychological theory (Woodger), the function of generalization (Arne Ness), the concept of Gestalt (Grelling and Oppenheim), the departmentalization of unified science (Neurath), propositional logic in the Middle Ages (K. Durr), the scope of empirical knowledge (Ayer), logic as a deductive theory (Waismann), two ways of definition by verification (Braithwaite), physics and logical empiricism (Frank), significant analysis of volitional language (Mannoury), and imperatives and logic (Joergensen).

The Harvard congress, the fifth and last congress before the war, was quite naturally attended predominantly by Americans, although some European philosophers and scientists were there. Further, in consequence of the anticultural and anti-Semitic politics of naziism, several of the leading figures of the movement had, in the course of the thirties, emigrated to the United States, which had thus become the new center of logical empiricism. The interest of the Americans had been stimulated by Morris and Nagel as well as by the men from Europe, among whom were Carnap, Reichenbach, Frank, von Mises, Feigl, Kaufmann, and Hempel. Some of the subjects of the papers read and discussed were: aims and methods for unifying science (Sarton, Bridgman, Kallen, Langer, Feigl, Nagel, Joergensen, von Mises, Gomperz), scientific method and the language of science (Swann, Carnap, Reichenbach, Hempel, Wundheiler, Williams, Senior, Felix Kaufmann, J. Kraft, Montague, Benjamin, Quine), methodology of the special sciences (Lindsay, Rougier, Pratt, Stevens, Leonard, Gerard, Henderson, Neurath, Morris,

Dennes, Somerville), problems in exact logic (Curry, Rosser-Kleene, Tarski, Church, Copeland, Margenau), science and society (Wirth, Zilsel, Brewster, Oboukhoff, Karpov, Byrne), and history of science (Jaeger, De Lacy, Santillana, Parsons, Davis, Kelsen, Frank). Although the outbreak of World War II, two days before the opening of this congress, made itself felt, the congress was carried through according to its program, and the lively and objective discussions of the subjects treated indicated a widespread interest in the views and methods of logical empiricism that promised well for the future of the movement in its new home. However, in consequence of the development of the war, and particularly when America joined in, conditions became so difficult that a slowing-down was inevitable. As I am yet uninformed as to details, I shall confine myself in the following exposition to the development of logical empiricism until the first of September, 1939, the date of the beginning of the war.

I shall, therefore, now go back to the twenties, or still further, and speak about the various circles with which the Vienna Circle gradually came to co-operate, owing to their common interest in one or several essential questions. They are principally the following: the Berlin group; the Lwow-Warsaw group; the Cambridge analysts, pragmatists, and operationalists; the Münster group, as well as various more isolated investigators in different countries.

2. The Berlin Group

Simultaneously with the gathering by Schlick of the Circle at Vienna, a similar group was formed in Berlin, which in 1928 was organized as the "Gesellschaft für empirische [later, following a proposal by David Hilbert, 'wissenschaftliche'] Philosophie." Among the leaders were Hans Reichenbach (born 1891), Alexander Herzberg, and Walter Dubislav; some other members of the society may be mentioned—Kurt Grelling (1886–1943?), Kurt Lewin (1890–1947), Wolfgang Köhler (born 1887), and Carl Gustav Hempel (born 1905). Its object was to promote scientific philosophy, by which was understood "a philosophical method which advances by analysis and criticism of the results of the special sciences to the stating of philosophical questions and their solutions."[4] The significance of such a scientific-analytical method had been emphasized by Reichenbach as early as 1920;[5] and, true to their program, he and those who agreed with him concerned themselves mainly with specific investigations of fundamental concepts, theories, and methods within the individual sciences, while they had some reservations about the tendency of the Vienna Circle to form systems and set up strict prescriptions and prohibitions.[6] Among their investigations may be mentioned Dubislav's detailed analysis of various methods of definition (*Über die Definition* [3d ed., 1926]); Grelling's inquiries into the paradoxes of the theory of sets and logic; Lewin's work on genidentity and scientific method; Köhler's on physical Gestalts; and Reichenbach's inquiries into the theory of relativity, the concepts of space and time, causality, probability, and the problem of induction. Being especially characteristic of the thought of the Berlin group, Reichenbach's work will be dealt with in more detail.

Through his inquiries into the general assumptions and the epistemological content of the theory of relativity, Reichenbach had reached the conclusion that the Kantian theory of the a priori character of space and time—as well as of other concepts of the natural and social sciences—was untenable. It is true that in his treatise on the theory of relativity and a priori knowledge he maintains that the world of experience is first constituted by means of a priori principles, but these are neither eternal nor deducible from an immanent scheme: "Our answer to the critical question is: there are, indeed, a priori principles which make the correlation of knowledge and observations univocal. But these may not be deduced from an immanent scheme. We must discover them only in the gradual labor of the analysis of science and cease questioning the duration of the validity of their special form."[7] In his remarkable work, *Philosophie der Raum-Zeit-Lehre* (1928), which contains a thorough epistemological analysis of the Euclidean and the non-Euclidean geometries and their relation to experience, he formulated the important principle of the relativity of geometry: "From this it follows that to say that a geometry is *true* is meaningless. We get only a proposition which characterizes something objective if, in addition to the geometry G of the space, we also specify the universal field of force K, which is connected with it. . . . Only the combination $G + K$ is an assertion of cognitive value."[8] This is partly due to the circumstance that all knowledge of reality presupposes so-called "correlative definitions" (*Zuordnungsdefinitionen*), i.e., statements as to what real things are designated by the concepts previously defined—a fact which had already been strongly stressed by Schlick in his *Allgemeine Erkenntnislehre* ([1918], pp. 55 f.) and by Reichenbach himself in his first book on the theory of relativity (pp. 32 f.). The first and most fundamental correlatives are a matter of definition and, in so far, arbitrary and of no epistemological value (which means that it is meaningless to regard them as true statements of the objects), but, on the basis of them, statements may be formulated, the truth and falsehood of which must be decided by experience. Formerly this fact was not fully realized, but the analysis of the theory of relativity has made it unambiguously clear "that correlative definitions are needed at many more places than the old theory of space-time believed; especially for the comparison of length at different places and in different inertial systems and for simultaneity. The core of the theory consists in the hypothesis that measuring bodies obey different correlative definitions from those which the classical theory of space-time assumed. This is, of course, an assertion of an empirical character and can be true or false; with it only the *physical theory of relativity* stands or falls. The *philosophical theory of relativity*, however, as the discovery of the definitional character of the system of measurement in all its particulars, is unaffected by any experience; to be sure, it was acquired through physical experiments; it is, however, a philosophical cognition, not subject to criticism from the special sciences."[9]

Unfortunately, it is impossible to enter into a detailed consideration of the many interesting and thorough analyses undertaken by Reichenbach in the work mentioned; and likewise space does not permit of a detailed account of his *Axiomatik der relativistischen Raum-Zeit-Lehre* (1924). However, a short exposition of his view on the relation between causality, probability, and induction is indispensable. His Doctor's thesis (1916) was *Der Begriff der Wahrscheinlichkeit für die mathematische Darstellung der Wirklichkeit*, and henceforth his interest has constantly centered on this subject, which he has treated in numerous papers and books, the most important of which are *Wahrscheinlichkeitslehre: Eine Untersuchung über die logischen und mathematischen Grundlagen der Wahrscheinlichkeitsrechnung* (1935) and *Experience and Prediction: An Analysis of the Foundations and the Structure of Knowledge* (1938). His fundamental thought is that natural science never confines itself merely to describing events of the past but also predicts coming events, which can never be done with absolute certainty but only with a smaller or greater degree of probability. The concept of probability, therefore, of necessity enters into the concept of knowledge of natural science. Even so-called "causal" statements are merely border cases of statements of probability: "For this reason, we must replace the strictly causal proposition by two propositions: (I) If an event is described by a certain number of parameters, a later event likewise characterized by a certain number of parameters can be predicted with probability p. (II) This probability p approaches 1 as more and more parameters are taken into consideration."[10] Accordingly, statements concerning the future are neither simply true nor simply false but more or less probable. In order to value their probability, a graduated scale for sentences must be constructed that, on the basis of previous facts, ascribes to every possible sentence about the future event a certain degree of truth. In the theory of statements concerning the future, two-valued logic, which operates only with the values truth and falsehood, should be replaced by a continuous scale of probability, and the theory of the Vienna Circle that the meaning of propositions consists in their method of verification should therefore be generalized; instead of maintaining that meaningful propositions must be either true or false, one should assert that they have a certain probability; and, instead of maintaining that propositions that are verified in the same way have the same meaning, one should assert that propositions to which any observable facts give the same value of probability have the same meaning. Only such a generalized probability-logic, containing two-valued logic as a boundary case, is capable of affording a satisfactory explanation of the statements of the natural and social sciences and their meaning. Reichenbach therefore developed a logic of probability, the basic concepts of which are definable by means of truth-tables that are generalizations of those of two-valued logic and contain these as special cases.[11] However, the basic elements of this probability-logic are not propositions but sequences of propositions, i.e., logical constructions obtained by co-ordinating with a propositional function a series of its arguments. In order to meet the difficulties arising when it is desired to fix the probability of a statement of a single future event, Reichenbach thinks it necessary to give a new interpretation of the meaning of statements of single events, and what he proposes is to assert such statements not as being true or false but as a "posit," the evaluation of which is fixed by the probability of the whole class of events of which the single event concerned is a member.[12] Having to choose among several relevant possibilities, we will choose the most probable and "posit" that one. The aim of the whole theory, which has been much debated and thoroughly discussed, is, then, in brief, to give an account of the meaning of a statement based not on its verifiability but on its probability, the latter being of such nature as to comprise verification and falsification as special cases. So far the theory has not, however, won the general assent of the adherents of logical empiricism.

The same applies to Reichenbach's theory of induction, which assumes that probability-logic can be applied to reality. But what right have we to assume that this is so? In answering this question Reichenbach attempts, first, to show that all the assumptions of probability-logic may be reduced to one, viz., the existence of a limit of relative frequency in a series of observable facts. If such limit exists, all the laws of the calculus of probability become tautological, and the question of the applicability of probability-logic is reduced to the question of whether the series of observable facts approach a limit or not. The assumption that they do so is decidedly no tautology, and already Hume has shown that the correctness of this assumption cannot be proved. In this Reichenbach agrees, but, arguing as follows, he still thinks there is a certain rational justification in maintaining the following assumption: Since we know neither whether the assumption is true nor whether it is false, we are justified in defending it in the same sense in which we make a "wager." We want to foresee the future, and we can do so if the assumption is justified—and so we wager on this assumption. Thus we have at least a *chance* of success, while, if we are skeptical and cautious and hold back, we are certain of obtaining nothing. "We are in the same situation as a man who wants to fish in an uncharted place in the sea. There is nobody to tell him whether or not there are fish in this place. Shall he cast his net? Well, if he wants to fish I would advise him to cast his net, at least to take the chance. It is preferable to try even in uncertainty than not to try and be certain of getting nothing."[13] This is his principal reply to the problem of induction, which he amplifies by considerations on the procedure of correction, according to which one does not merely consider a single series of inductions but connects it with the largest possible number of affiliated series, whereby it becomes possible to construct probabilities of higher order, which may increase the chance in every single case.[14] "The chances of our catching fish increase with the use of a more finely meshed net; we ought therefore to use such a net even if we do not know whether there are fish in the water or not. In these reflections, I submit, the problem of induction finds its solution. It does not presuppose a synthetic *a priori*, as Kant believed; for our characterization of induction as a necessary condition of prediction as well as the technique of refining inductive conclusions by the process of correction can be deduced from pure mathematics, that is, with tautological transformations only. This solution is due to a reinterpretation of the nature and meaning of scientific systems. A scientific system is not maintained as true, but only as our best wager on the future. To discover what is our *best* wager in any situation of inquiry is the aim of all scientific toil; never can we arrive at predictions which are certain. Science is the net we cast into the stream of events; whether fish will be caught with it, whether facts will correspond to it, does not depend on our work alone. We work and wait—if without success, well then, our work was in vain."[15]

The work of the Berlin group came to an end when the Nazis came into power in 1933. Its members were dispersed; some of them died, and others emigrated to the United States, where a number of them, including Reichenbach, R. von Mises, and Hempel, are continuing their work in the analysis of science.

3. The Lwow-Warsaw Group[16]

Under the influence of Kazimierz Twardowski (1866–1938), a pupil of Brentano, a vigorous opposition arose in Poland against the irrationalistic metaphysics of the Polish romanticists. Members of this opposition who should be mentioned are: Jan Lukasiewicz (born 1878), Tadeusz Kotarbinski (born 1886), Stanislaw Lesniewski (1886–1939), Zygmunt Zawirski (1882–1946), Kasimierz Ajdukiewicz (born 1890) and Leon Chwistek (1884–1944); and among the younger ones were: Alfred Tarski (born 1901), Janina Hosiasson-Lindenbaum (1899–1941), Mordechaj Wajsberg (died 1942?), Adolf Lindenbaum (died 1941), Marja Kokoszynska, Stanislaw Jaskowski, Izydora Dambska, Henryk Mehlberg, Edward Poznański, Alexander Wundheiler, M. Presburger, and Boleslaw Sobocinski. These investigators were almost all well trained in symbolic logic, and several of them have made valuable contributions to the development of this discipline. Although none of them were adherents of logical positivism, several of them began, in the thirties, to co-operate closely with the Vienna Circle in the scientific analytic work in which they were keenly interested and which they pursued under the name of "metatheory," i.e., the theory of scientific theories. There was an especially lively and fruitful exchange of thought between Carnap and Gödel, on the one side, and Tarski, on the other. In this connection attention should be drawn to

Tarski's important treatise, "Der Wahrheitsbegriff in den Sprachen der deduktiven Disciplinen" (in German in *Studia philosophica*, I.[Lwow, 1935]; in Polish in *Travaux de la société de sciences*, Cl. III, No. 34 [Warsaw, 1933]). In this he showed that the truth-concept in formal languages may be defined purely morphologically, i.e., solely by means of the external forms of the expressions and their relations, but that this definition presupposes a metalanguage, containing expressions of a higher logical type than the language whose truth-concept is being defined. Further, Tarski demonstrated that the semantics (i.e., the theory of the relation between signs and their designata) of any formalized language can be built up as a deductive theory with its own axioms and its own fundamental concepts based on the morphology of the language alone. That such investigations were bound to be of the greatest importance to the further development of logical empiricism will appear from the subsequent exposition of Carnap's view of philosophy as the syntactical and, later also, the semantical analysis of the language of science.

4. Pragmatists and Operationalists[17]

In America the development of pragmatism had led to a philosophical view resembling the general viewpoints of European logical empiricism in many respects and well suited to form a natural supplement to them. In Charles Sanders Peirce (1839–1914) we find the combination of an interest in empiricist philosophy and symbolic logic that is characteristic of the movement. Even Wittgenstein's theory of the meaning of propositions consisting in their verifiability was in a way anticipated by Peirce: "It appears, then, that the rule for attaining the third grade of clearness of apprehension is as follows: consider what effects, which might conceivably have practical bearings, we conceive the object of our conception to have. Then, our conception of these effects is the whole of our conception of the object."[18] Although this rule was considered principally with reference to morals and religion by William James (1842–1910), other American investigators used it in a purely epistemological way. This is seen most clearly in the so-called "operationalists," whose most prominent representative is P. W. Bridgman, the physicist, who says in his *The Logic of Modern Physics* (1927): "In general, we mean by any concept nothing more than a set of operations; *the concept is synonymous with the corresponding set of operations.* If the concept is physical, as of length, the operations are actual physical operations, namely those by which length is measured; or if the concept is mental, as of mathematical continuity, the operations are mental operations, namely those by which we determine whether a given aggregate of magnitudes is continuous . . . the concepts can be defined only in the range of actual experiment, and are undefined and meaningless in regions as yet untouched by experiments. . . . Of course the true meaning of a term is to be found by observing what a man does with it, not by what he says about it."[19] This point of view, which puts the main stress on the practice and the acts of the investigator during his work of investigation, is characteristic of the whole pragmatic attitude. The way in which it was developed by John Dewey (born 1859) in, for instance, his *How We Think* (1910) and in *Experience and Nature* (1925) and *Logic, the Theory of Inquiry* (1939) gave this attitude a decidedly biosocial character that made the adoption of behavioristic viewpoints natural. In George Herbert Mead's (1863–1931) *Mind, Self, and Society* (1934) and *Philosophy of the Act* (1938), this tendency became dominant. By emphasizing the social nature of language and science, pragmatism led to a concept of meaning which, in Charles Morris' words, may be briefly stated as follows: "Seen in terms of the context of social behavior, meaning always involves a set of expectations aroused by the symbolic functioning of some object, while the object meant, whether past, present, or future, and whether confrontable by a particular person or not, is any object which satisfies the expectations. A self, as a social being, can for instance expect that other selves will verify its own expectations (a situation of constant occurrence in science), and in this sense at least meaning can outrun personal verification."[20] This view Morris himself later developed into a *semiotic* theory, according to which the meaning-situation is an organic whole with three closely interrelated dimensions: "the relation of sign to objects will be called M_E (to be read, 'the existential dimension of meaning,' or, in short, 'existential meaning'); the psychological, biological and sociological aspects of the significatory process will be designated M_P ('the pragmatic dimension of meaning,' or 'pragmatic meaning'); the syntactical relations to other symbols within the language will be symbolized by M_F ('the formal dimension of meaning,' or 'formal meaning'). The meaning of a sign is thus the sum of its meaning-dimensions: $M = M_E + M_P + M_F$."[21] Whereas the older form of empiricism concerned itself mainly with the first, pragmatism with the second, and logical positivism with the third of these dimensions of meaning, Morris thinks that, by considering all of them equally, a synthesis may be reached which signifies at the same time an expansion of the concept of meaning and an associated extended form of empiricism which he calls "scientific empiricism."

Of other American investigators working on related pragmatistic-operationalistic-scientific-analytic lines, among the best known are the following: Clarence Irving Lewis (born 1883), developed in his *Mind and the World Order* (1929) a "conceptualistic pragmatism" and undertook in his *Symbolic Logic* (1932), which he wrote together with C. H. Langford, significant investigations concerning the logic of modality; Morris R. Cohen (1880–1946), strongly influenced by Russell, expounded in his *Reason and Nature* (1931) a "realistic rationalism"; Victor F. Lenzen gave, in *The Nature of Physical Theory* (1931), an enlightening analysis of the concepts and theories of physics, emphasizing the importance of "successive definitions." Numerous other American philosophers and special scientists have worked along lines more or less related to the viewpoints of logical empiricism without having been in direct contact with this movement. Among its other adherents should be mentioned Ernest Nagel, A. E. Blumberg, Daniel J. Bronstein, and other members of the Harvard congress, and we must add to these the logical empiricists who have emigrated from Europe.

5. The Uppsala School[22]

Although the contact between logical empiricism and the members of the Uppsala school has so far been comparatively slight, this distinctive trend within Swedish philosophy should be mentioned because it is, in several essential respects, closely related to logical empiricism and because the connection between the two seems to be growing. The Uppsala school was founded about 1910 by Axel Hägerström (1868–1939) and his colleague Adolf Phalén (1864–1931) and gathered a number of adherents and pupils, among whom were: Karl Hedvall, Harry Meurling, Ejnar Tegen, Vilhelm Lundstedt, Karl Olivecrona, Gunnar Oxenstjerna, Konrad Marc-Wogau, Ingemar Hedenius, and Anders Wedberg. Although the reasoning and the views of the two movements are not identical, there is a far-reaching agreement between the Uppsala school and logical empiricism, in that they are both decidedly antimetaphysical and for both the main task of philosophy consists in the analysis of concepts. Further, both are opposed to epistemological idealism ("subjectivism," the nature and existence of that which is conceived depends on our conception thereof) and are adherents of the theory that statements of valuations are not true statements but merely expressions of certain feelings and, accordingly, have no factual meaning. Especially with regard to the two last points, the Uppsala school has performed a comprehensive and commendable piece of work which historically anticipates the work of logical empiricism without, however, having influenced it. As has already been mentioned, a certain contact was established during the course of the thirties, and there is every reason to expect a closer co-operation between the two movements to their mutual inspiration and a further development of the basic views. In this connection Marc-Wogau's recent study, *Die Theorie der Sinnesdaten: Probleme der neueren Erkenntnistheorie in England* (1945), should be mentioned.

6. The Münster Group

As the last of the groups working with logical empiricism, the logistic school in Münster, created by Heinrich Scholz (born

1884), may be mentioned. Scholz, who worked originally in theology and philosophy of religion, became interested in logistics; and in the thirties he inspired a number of young investigators —Bachmann, Hermes, and others—to undertake significant inquiries into the foundations of logic and mathematics, while he himself was eagerly engaged in the study of the historical development of logic, stressing in particular the work of Leibniz and Frege (*Geschichte der Logik* [1931]). He was not an adherent of the ideas of logical empiricism, and the co-operation was strictly limited to formalistic-logistic problems, with no mention of the positivistic applications and viewpoints condemned in Nazi Germany. Scholz and his school have resumed their work since the war.

7. Individuals

Besides the above-mentioned groups entering into a limited or extensive collaboration with logical empiricists, there were in the various countries a number of individuals who joined the movement and took an active part in its development. Among these were the following: Eino Kaila (born 1890 in Finland), developed logistic-empiricistic ideas in a series of remarkable writings (such as, for instance, *Über den physikalischen Realitätsbegriff* [1942]) and expounded his theory of knowledge based on those ideas in his *Den mänskliga Kunskapen* (1939); his pupil, Georg Henrik von Wright, besides making intensive studies in *The Logical Problems of Induction* (1941) and *Über Wahrscheinlichkeit* (1945), also wrote a simple and lucid exposition of the fundamental thought of logical empiricism (*Den logiska Empirismen* [1943]); the Frenchman, Louis Rougier (born 1889), has published writings on *Les Paralogismes du rationalisme* (1920), on *La Structure des théories deductives* (1921), on *La Scolastique et le thomisme* (1925), and various other subjects of scientific theory; the Englishman, J. H. Woodger, after having undertaken an epistemological analysis of biological concepts and theories in his *Biological Principles* (1929), has made valuable contributions to the development of formal theories with biological interpretations in his *Axiomatic Method in*

Biology (1937) and in his monograph in this *Encyclopedia* entitled *The Technique of Theory Construction;* Alfred Jules Ayer (also English), in his *Language, Truth, and Logic* (1936), gave a penetrating exposition of the fundamental principles and main results of logical empiricism and in numerous articles and papers defended them against various English critics. Later he expounded the theory in a revised form in his *The Foundations of Empirical Knowledge* (1940). In Germany, P. Oppenheim dealt with the systematization of science and (together with C. G. Hempel) wrote *Der Typusbegriff im Lichte der neuen Logik* (1936). The Swiss, F. Gonseth, formed an "idoneistic" theory of his own concerning the nature of mathematics; and Karl Dürr dealt with the logic of Leibniz and other historical predecessors of some of the fundamental thoughts of logical empiricism. The Norwegian, Arne Ness (born 1912), put forward a behavioristic theory of knowledge in terms referring to the verbal and nonverbal behavior of the scientist (*Erkenntnis und wissenschaftliches Verhalten* [1936]). In his work '*Truth' as Conceived by Those Who Are Not Professional Philosophers* (1938), he studied the actual use of the term 'truth' by psychological methods (questionnaires and interviews). He later developed a special form of philosophical analysis of language which he calls "precision analysis." It is elaborated in his forthcoming work, *Interpretation and Preciseness*. The Dane, Joergen Joergensen (born 1894), has written *A Treatise of Formal Logic*, Volumes I–III (1931), as well as a survey of the various sciences in their systematic contexts from encyclopedic points of view, and has used logical-empiristic viewpoints and methods in his *Psykologi paa biologisk Grundlag* ("Psychology Based on Biology") (1941–45).

Many other investigators in various countries have in various fields worked more or less along the lines of logical empiricism: the philosopher B. von Juhos in Austria, the logistician Uuno Saarnio in Finland, and, in Denmark, Alf Ross and Bent Schultzer, professors of law, and the sociologist, Svend Ranulf. It is impossible to make this an inclusive list because there is difficulty in deciding just where to draw the line.

8. The Question of the Nature of Philosophy

After this outline of the external development of logical empiricism, I shall now consider its internal development. As has already been indicated, important divergencies arose toward the end of the twenties within the Vienna Circle because of various doubts as to some of its own presuppositions. These divergencies concerned the question as to how their philosophical work should be rightly characterized on the basis of their own principles, on the question of the verifiability of statements, and, accordingly, on the theory of meaning as synonymous with verifiability.

As to the nature of philosophy, Wittgenstein maintained that the task of philosophy is a clarification of thought, not a theory but an activity, and that philosophical propositions are, strictly speaking, logically meaningless and "inexpressible," for which reason they should be discarded when their purpose has been attained, in the same way as a scaffolding is thrown away when a building is completed. While, to begin with, Schlick and most of the other members of the Vienna Circle immediately accepted this view, Neurath raised strong opposition against it toward the end of the twenties, as he feared that it would lead to a revival of metaphysics as "the philosophy of the inexpressible." In this he was strongly supported by Carnap, who gave the objections a precise form and put forward a new view of the nature of philosophy that was clearly expressed in his article "On the Character of Philosophical Problems."[23] According to Carnap, *philosophy is the theory of science* or *"the logic of science,* i.e., the logical analysis of the concepts, propositions, proofs, theories of science,"* and its propositions are not meaningless mediums for elucidation but constitute a legitimate field of study, which he called the "logical syntax of the language of science" and treated in detail in his great work *Logische Syntax der Sprache* (1934),[24] which we shall now consider.

9. Carnap's Logical Syntax of Language*

Carnap's concept of the logical syntax of a language is a generalization of Hilbert's metamathematics, in which, as is well known, the meaning of mathematical signs and formulas is completely disregarded and they are considered solely in a "formalistic" way, i.e., as figures written down and transformed according to certain definite rules. In other words, metamathematics is a theory the object of which is mathematical signs and formulas. Similarly, the logical syntax of language is a purely formal theory of the linguistic signs and their composition into sentences, proofs, and theories, particularly a theory of the signs or sign combinations occurring or acceptable in the sciences, including, of course, those occurring in mathematics; for this reason Carnap's syntax comprises Hilbert's metamathematics as a special part. While it was the object of Hilbert to establish through metamathematics the consistency of classical mathematics, Carnap's purpose is not so much to prove that all science is noncontradictory as to establish the following two theses: (*a*) an investigation of the logic of science need never pay regard to the meaning but only to the formal rules of linguistic expressions, and (*b*) the fixation of the formal rules of any language and the investigation of the consequences of such rules can be built up in exactly the same way as a scientific theory, namely, as a logical syntax of the language concerned, and can usually be formulated in that very language. Thus, considering philosophy as the syntax of the language of science, Carnap refutes Wittgenstein's view of philosophy as an activity that is able only to express itself in meaningless sentences; and at the same time he sharply delimits philosophy as something apart from the special sciences, since philosophy does not deal with the *objects* but only with the *sentences about the objects of such sciences*. The special sciences comprise all "object-questions," whereas philosophy is concerned only with the "logical questions" dealing with scientific concepts, propositions, the-

* [In fairness to Professor Joergensen it should be stated that considerations of space made it necessary to omit portions of the analysis of Carnap's earlier views.— THE EDITORS.]

ories, etc., considered formally as complexes of signs constructed in accordance with certain rules for combinations of signs. These rules are partly rules of formation, partly rules of transformation. The former are the rules for the composition of the various kinds of signs of a language into sentences (i.e., corresponding roughly to usual grammar); the latter are rules for the deduction of a sentence from other sentences (i.e., rules of inference, so that the logical syntax will comprise what is generally called "logic"). For the different (from a logical point of view) languages, these two kinds of rules are different and may be fixed arbitrarily, because they, so to speak, define the language to which they are to apply. Here the "principle of tolerance" applies: "*It is not our business to set up prohibitions, but to arrive at conventions. . . . In logic, there are no morals.* Everyone is at liberty to build up his own logic, i.e. his own form of language, as he wishes. All that is required of him is that, if he wishes to discuss it, he must state his methods clearly, and give syntactical rules instead of philosophical arguments."[25] Thus we may, for instance, construct one language restricted to finitist mathematics and another language the mathematical part of which contains all of classical mathematics (and physics), and so reduce any dispute between intuitionists and formalists in mathematics to a mere disagreement as to which form of language they wish to use.

Carnap then proceeds to illustrate the syntax by means of two languages serving as instances of formal languages. Since it is a very complicated matter, although in principle possible, to set up the formal rules of our everyday language, Carnap chooses two artificial languages, viz., the language of finitist mathematics and the language of classical mathematics. He calls them "language I" and "language II," formulates the syntactical rules for each, and shows that the syntax of language I can be expressed in that language itself, so there is nothing to prevent a language in this sense describing its own form or structure (which had been declared impossible by Wittgenstein). Carnap demonstrates this by means of the method of arithmetization, introduced by Gödel into metamathematics, according to which a number is co-ordinated to every sign of the system in such a way that every expression can be translated into a corresponding arithmetical expression. And as language I contains arithmetic, this means that the syntax of this language can be expressed in the language itself.

In his investigation of the two model languages Carnap states a number of instances worked out in detail and confirming the above-mentioned thesis *b*. But, however thoroughly and subtly worked out, instances cannot, of course, prove the thesis generally, and Carnap accordingly undertakes a series of fundamental inquiries into general syntax, i.e., into syntactical rules concerning either all languages or comprehensive classes of languages. In these he defines and discusses a number of logical-syntactical concepts—the most important is the concept of "consequence," which for any language is defined by the rules of transformation of that language and which, therefore, varies from one language to another. Roughly speaking, it may be said that a sentence in a given language is a consequence of certain other sentences if, and only if, it can be constructed from these latter by application of the rules of transformation of the language concerned. As the rules of transformation are purely formal, the concept of "consequence" is so, too, and by means of the latter it is then possible to define various other important syntactical concepts, such as the concepts "analytic," "contradictory," and "synthetic," which give an exhaustive classification of all sentences occurring in the different branches of science, and also the concept "the content of a sentence," besides many other concepts that are worked out with extreme penetration and mathematical precision. For that very reason they are too complicated to be stated here, but an impression of Carnap's way of procedure may perhaps be obtained by considering his simple and lucid exposition in *Philosophy and Logical Syntax* (1935).

"Given any language-system, or set of formation rules and transformation rules, among the sentences of this language there will be true and false sentences. But we cannot define the terms 'true' and 'false' in syntax, because whether a given sentence is true or false will generally depend not only upon the syntactical form of the sentence but also upon experience; that is to say, upon something extra-linguistic. It may be, however, that in certain cases a sentence is true or false only by reason of the rules of the language. Such sentences we will call *valid* and *contravalid* respectively. Our definition of validity is as follows: a sentence is called *valid*, if it is a consequence of the null class of premises (i.e. if it presupposes no premise) . . . a sentence 'A' of a certain language-system is called *contravalid* if every sentence of this system is a consequence of 'A'. . . ."[26]

By means of the concepts here defined it is then possible to give a purely formal definition of the "sense" or "content" of a sentence. "If we wish to characterize the purport of a given sentence, its content, its assertive power, so to speak, we have to regard the class of those sentences which are consequences of the given sentence. Among these consequences we may leave aside the valid sentences, because they are consequences of every sentence. We define therefore as follows: the class of the non-valid consequences of a given sentence is called the *content* of this sentence."[27] The logical-philosophical significance of such definitions is that they show that all factual sentences may be submitted, by means of them, to a logical analysis without its being necessary at any point to consider anything but the purely formal properties of the sentences concerned. Their "sense" in the usual vague and undefined meaning of the word is logically irrelevant and may be replaced, according to Carnap's theory, in all logical investigations by the formal concept of "content" here defined.

There are, however, certain sentences with regard to which this is anything but evident, and as to these Carnap proceeds in a special way. They are the sentences which he calls "pseudo-object-sentences," i.e., sentences which *seem* to deal with the objects mentioned in them but which, upon a closer inspection, appear to be purely syntactical (e.g., 'The rose is a thing'). As these very sentences play an important part in current philosophy, Carnap attaches considerable weight to them, it being possible to maintain his above-mentioned thesis *a* only if it can be established that the pseudo-object-sentences are syntactical in character. He contrasts them with the *syntactical sentences* mentioned above and with *real object-sentences* (e.g., 'the rose is red'), which concern extra-linguistic objects and belong to the special sciences.

Although a pseudo-object-sentence may have the same grammatical subject as an object-sentence, it asserts no quality of the subject. We can, moreover, discover its truth without observing the object to which we refer but only by considering its syntactical status. Thus we see that a pseudo-object-sentence is really syntactical and can be translated into a syntactical sentence having the same content (e.g., 'The word 'rose' is a thing-word').

Syntactical sentences are also said to be sentences of *the formal mode of speech*, while pseudo-object-sentences are said to be sentences of *the material mode of speech*. According to Carnap, the material mode of speech often gives rise to pseudo-problems or disputes that may be avoided by translating the sentences concerned into the formal mode of speech.[28] Indeed, all traditional metaphysical problems seem to arise from the very circumstance that they have been discussed in the material mode of speech instead of having been analyzed syntactically. An example will illustrate this: "One frequent cause of dispute amongst philosophers is the question what *things* really are. The representative of a positivistic school asserts: 'A thing is a complex of sense-data.' His realistic adversary replies: 'No, a thing is a complex of physical matter'; and an endless and futile argument is thus begun. Yet both of them are right after all: the controversy has arisen only on account of the unfortunate use of the material mode. Let us translate the two theses into the formal mode. That of the positivist becomes: 'Every sentence containing a thing-designation is equipollent* with a class of sentences which contain no thing-designations, but sense-data-designations,' which is true; the transformation into sense-data-references has often been shown in epistemology. That of the realist takes the form: 'Every sentence containing a thing-designation

* Two sentences are *equipollent* if each is a consequence of the other.

is equipollent with a sentence containing no thing-designation, but space-time-coordinates and physical functions,' which is obviously also true. . . . There is no inconsistency. In the original formulation in the material mode the theses *seemed* to be incompatible, because they *seemed* to concern the essence of things, both of them having the form: 'A thing is such and such.' "[29]

In other cases the problem is solved by our showing that apparently contradictory theses do not belong to the same syntactically defined language. This applies, for instance, to the controversy between the logicists (Frege, Russell) and the axiomaticists (Peano, Hilbert) on the nature of numbers. The former assert: "Numbers are classes of classes of things," while the latter assert: "Numbers are a unique kind of entities." Translating these assertions into the formal mode, we get: "Numerical symbols are class-symbols of the second order," and "Numerical symbols are symbols of individuals (i.e., symbols of zero order that occur only as arguments)." These sentences may be conceived either as belonging each to its own separate arithmetical language or as proposals for separate languages, i.e., for different ways of talking about numbers. In either case the discussion is no longer a controversy about what is true and what is false but is reduced to a question of what language is best suited for talking about arithmetics.

On the basis of similar analyses of a long series of philosophical problems and assertions of various kinds, Carnap thinks himself justified in asserting that all the theorems of philosophy can be treated syntactically, that is to say, can be translated into the formal mode of speech whereby the problems attached to them will either be automatically revealed as being illusory pseudo-problems or be reduced to proposals for different languages, the expediency, but not the correctness, of which may be discussed. He finds no need to eliminate completely the material mode of speech: "This mode is usual and perhaps sometimes suitable. But it must be handled with special caution. In all decisive points of discussion it is advisable to replace the material by the formal mode; and in using the formal mode, reference to the language-system must not be neglected. It is not necessary that the thesis should refer to a language-system already put forward; it may sometimes be desired to formulate a thesis on the basis of a so far unknown language-system, which is to be characterized by just this thesis. In such a case the thesis is not an assertion, but a proposal or project, in other words a part of the definition of the designed language-system. If one partner in a philosophical discussion cannot or will not give a translation of his thesis into the formal mode, or if he will not state to which language-system his thesis refers, then the other will be well-advised to refuse the debate, because the thesis of his opponent is incomplete, and discussion would lead to nothing but empty wrangling."[30]

The main result is, therefore, that every indicative, meaningful sentence either is an object-sentence which, as such, belongs to one special science or another or is a syntactical sentence which belongs to logic or mathematics, and that, accordingly, philosophy may be defined as the sum total of the true syntactical sentences concerning the languages of the special sciences. This again leads to various new problems—or old problems in a new formulation—such as: Do the various special sciences speak the same language, and, if not, is it possible to construct a language common to all? And what is the criterion of the truth—or merely meaningfulness—of an object-sentence? The first of these questions leads to the discussion of one of the main points of logical empiricism: *the unity of science* and the associated thesis of *physicalism*, while the second is important with regard to the *theory of verifiability* and to the problem of the *basis of the system of constituion*. As these problems oveilap to a large extent, a constant interaction took place in their treatment from the beginning of the thirties; but, for the purposes of clarity, they will here, as far as possible, be treated separately, and we shall start with the last problem: the problem of basis and verification.

10. Protocol-Sentences and Substantiations ("Konstatierungen")

In his *Der logische Aufbau der Welt* Carnap had, as we know, chosen as basis for his theory of constitution the immediately given experiences which he asserted were subjectless. This starting point was not, however, acceptable to Neurath. He was afraid that it might lead to a return to metaphysical absolutism, and, besides, he found the connection between the experiences and the sentences that were to describe them, and to be checked by them, metaphysical.

He consequently maintained that propositions were checked only by other propositions. A new proposition is compared with those already accepted and is called correct if it can be incorporated into the system. Sometimes one may, although this decision is not easily made, change the whole previously accepted system of propositions to allow for the new one. "Within unified science there are significant tasks of transformations,"[31] whereas *outside* unified science there is nothing with which a relation may be established. Not even direct statements of observation can be compared with the objects concerned but merely with other statements of observation or with statements of other kinds, and their truth does not depend on their agreement with the objects observed but solely on their agreement with the totality of all statements accepted at the given time. Neurath now proceeded to look for purely formal, syntactical characteristics of direct statements of observation, which he called (following a suggestion of Carnap) *protocol-sentences*, as he wanted to stress that these sentences were of the same kind as the ones which natural scientists use in making protocols (records of observations) and which form the starting point for their hypotheses and theories and the criterion for their validity.

As the debate proceeded, the prevailing view became that from a philosophical-epistemological standpoint there was no difference in principle between protocol-sentences and other legitimate scientific sentences; and the discussion concerning the syntactical form of protocol-sentences therefore subsided, the whole question then being considered a matter of convention.

The above "most radical form" of logical empiricism did not, however, win the general approval of all the followers of the movement. Schlick was in direct opposition. He maintained that, by introducing the concept "protocol-sentence," the aim had been from the beginning to sort out a group of sentences capable of serving as an absolutely firm basis for knowledge and as a means of testing all other sentences. And, since noncontradictoriness or incorporability in a system of sentences cannot enable us to distinguish between knowledge of reality and fairy tales that are consistently built up, the sentences characteristic of knowledge must be distinguished by special properties. But, as he admits that even protocol-sentences are hypothetical because for various reasons they *may* be doubted (the observer may, for instance, be guilty of a slip of the pen, or he may have lied) and are sometimes rejected (as, for instance, a single measurement that cannot be brought to agree with a certain series of measurements of the same magnitude), he thinks that knowledge—certain knowledge—cannot be based on protocol-sentences but must be based on certain sentences of observations or "Konstatierungen," by which he understands statements of what is being observed. These are always of the form "so-and-so here now." What these sentences have in common is that they fulfil the function of pointing. What 'here' and 'now', etc., mean cannot generally be given in verbal definitions but must be specified by gesture, pointing, etc. The meaning of a substantiation can be understood if, and only if, it is compared with the facts. However, as in the case of analytic judgments, establishing the meaning of a substantiation is not distinguishable from establishing its truth. "It makes as little sense to ask whether I can be mistaken about its truth as about that of a tautology. Both are absolutely valid. However, the analytic, tautological sentence is without content, while the substantiation provides us the satisfaction of genuine knowledge of fact."[32] Strictly speaking, however, substantiations cannot be written down at all, because when we do so the "pointing" words 'here' and 'now' lose their sense.[33]

Against this view Neurath asked how it would ever be possible to ascertain that Schlick had had an experience which he could not write down[34] and also called attention to the fact that the absolutely certain knowledge sought by Schlick is not an empirical fact but wishful thinking connected with certain metaphysical ideas of a difference between "the real world" and knowledge of it. Referring to the detailed and penetrating criticism of this metaphysical duplication which Frank had set forth in his *Das Kausalgesetz und seine Grenzen* (1932), chapter x, Neurath said: "Thus the attempt to achieve knowledge of fact is reduced to the attempt to bring the sentences of science into agreement with as many protocol-sentences as possible."[35] And as to consistent fairy tales versus knowledge of reality, he refers to the fact that "the practice of life" very quickly reduces the number of the systems of sentences having an equal right *from a logical point of view,* as most of them soon appear unsuited for predictions.[36] But this does not make the rest absolutely certain. *"There is no way to make absolutely certain protocol-sentences the point of departure for the sciences."* There is no *tabula rasa.* We are like sailors who have to rebuild their ship on the open sea without ever being able to tear it down in a dry dock to rebuild it with new parts.[37]

As to the further course of this discussion, which was cut short by the death of Schlick in 1936, readers are referred to the instructive articles by C. G. Hempel, "On the Logical Positivists' Theory of Truth"[38] and "Some Remarks on 'Facts' and Propositions,"[39] in which he defends the standpoint of Neurath and Carnap and criticizes that of Schlick. It is impossible here to go into details, but a single aspect of the matter, namely, the development of the question of verifiability, will be dealt with below, as it signifies an essential generalization of the logical-empiricist view of the truth and meaning of sentences.

11. Verifiability and Testability

Keeping in mind that logical positivists identified the meaningfulness of reality-sentences with their verifiability, it will be understood that the question of how reality-sentences can be verified must be of the utmost interest to them. Reality-sentences that cannot be verified or falsified are, according to this view, meaningless. But now it became apparent that not even protocol-sentences, by means of which the truth of all other reality-sentences was to be tested, were capable of being verified in the strict sense of the word so that they become absolutely certain. And matters are still worse, of course, with regard to more complicated sentences, as, for instance, the general sentences of which the natural laws form a part, since from a logical point of view they are "general implications" in the simplest case of the form: for all x, if x has the property f, then x has the property g. As Popper says, "logical positivism destroys not only metaphysics but also natural science."[40] As a first way out of this difficulty Schlick had proposed a different conception of natural laws: "Natural laws are not (in the language of the logician) 'general implications,' because they cannot be verified for *all* cases; they are rather rules or directions for the investigator to find his way through the real world, to discover true sentences, to predict certain occurrences."[41] This way of escape, however, had not won the approval of the other logical empiricists, who felt bound to acknowledge natural laws as general implications. But how then could they be made to agree with the theory that the meaningfulness of sentences consists in their verifiability?

This could be done only by amending the theory. A first proposal in that direction was made by Popper in his *Logik der Forschung* (1935), where, as the criterion of the meaningfulness of a sentence, he uses not the verifiability but the falsifiability of the sentence. "Our formulation depends on an asymmetrical relation between verifiability and falsifiability, which is connected with the logical form of universal sentences; viz., these are never derivable from particular sentences but can be contradicted by particular sentences."[42] By this criterion of meaning, he proposed to sort out empirical-scientific sentences from a priori–analytical sentences (logic and mathematics) as well as from nonfalsifiable reality-sentences (metaphysics). But this suggestion was not approved either because universal sentences, logically viewed, seem to parallel existential sentences, which latter can never be falsified but in certain cases may be verified, and because some scientifically recognized sentences contain a combination of the peculiarities of universal and existential sentences (they contain both a universal and an existential quantifier) and, accordingly, can be neither verified nor falsified. This applies, for example, to statements concerning the limit of the relative frequency of a certain event in a series of events, that is, concerning probability-statements according to a commonly held view. Some logical empiricists were for a time inclined to regard these statements as "pseudo-sentences," or they sought another interpretation of sentences of probability. As this gave rise to great difficulties, the view was gradually accepted that scientific sentences may very well contain both universal and existential quantifiers, and consequently it became necessary to look for a new and more liberal criterion of meaning than that mentioned above. As he had done so often before, Carnap pulled the loose ends together, worked the matter through, and outlined a theory and a proposal that have since formed the starting point for the further discussion of this problem.

Carnap's exposition was published in a treatise called "Testability and Meaning."[43] Popper, in his *Logik der Forschung*, had strongly emphasized the necessity of distinguishing between various "degrees of testability (*Prüfbarkeit*)"; and Carnap, at the congress in Paris (1935), had stressed the importance of distinguishing between "truth" and "confirmation" (*Bewährung*): while truth is an absolute concept independent of time, confirmation is a relative concept, the degrees of which vary with the development of science at any given time. Further, he distinguished between two different kinds of reality-sentences, viz., those that are directly testable and those that are merely indirectly testable. "By a directly testable sentence we mean one for which, under imaginable conditions, on the basis of one or a few observations, we can with confidence regard either as so strongly confirmed that we accept it or as so strongly disconfirmed that we reject it. . . . Indirect testing of a sentence consists in directly testing other sentences which have a certain relation to it."[44] The most important testing operations are (a) confrontation of a sentence with observation and (b) confrontation of the sentence with sentences that have been previously recognized. Of these, the former operations are the more important, for in their absence there is no confirmation at all, while the latter are merely auxiliary operations, which mostly serve to eliminate unsuited sentences from the system of sentences of the science concerned.

These views are now further implemented and defined in "Testability and Meaning," which contains the following introductory remarks: "If by verification is meant a definitive and final establishment of truth, then no (synthetic) sentence is ever verifiable, as we shall see. We can only confirm a sentence more and more. Therefore we shall speak of the problem of *confirmation* rather than of the problem of verification. We distinguish the *testing* of a sentence from its confirmation, thereby understanding a procedure—e.g. the carrying out of certain experiments—which leads to a confirmation in some degree either of the sentence itself or of its negation. We shall call a sentence *testable* if we know such a method of testing for it; and we shall call it *confirmable* if we know under what conditions the sentence would be confirmed. As we shall see, a sentence may be confirmable without being testable; e.g. if we know that our observation of such and such a course of events would confirm the sentence, and such and such a different course would confirm its negation without knowing how to set up either this or that observation."[45]

Reichenbach thinks he has found a measure for the degree of confirmation in the limit of the relative frequency of the cases of confirmation, so that any sentence may be said to be a probability-sentence; this being a controversial point, however, Carnap prefers to distinguish between probability (in the frequency sense) and degree of confirmation;[46] he also advises us not to discuss matters in the material mode of speech, as this mode serves to veil the fact that the answering of certain pertinent questions depends on the choice of the structure of the language applied, which appears evident when the formal mode of speech is used. He therefore develops a logical-syntactical analysis of the pertinent concepts, which is too technical to be quoted here. It must suffice to state that the investigation results in various proposals or requirements, the fulfilment of which signifies more or less radical forms of empiricism and may be said to define different concepts of what empiricism is or should be. He makes four requirements in all, of which the first is the most rigid and the last the most liberal one. Being formulated in the formal mode of speech, the requirements concerned define four different empiricist languages. The four requirements are as follows:

"*Requirement of Complete Testability:* Every synthetic sentence must be completely testable." I.e., if any synthetic sentence S is given, we must know a method of testing for every descriptive predicate occurring in S.[47]

"*Requirement of Complete Confirmability:* Every synthetic sentence must be completely confirmable." I.e., if any synthetic sentence S is given, there must be for every descriptive predicate occurring in S the possibility of our finding out for suitable points whether or not they have the property designated by the predicate in question.[48]

"*Requirement of Testability:* Every synthetic sentence must be testable." This requirement admits incompletely testable sentences—these are chiefly universal sentences to be confirmed incompletely by their instances.[49]

"*Requirement of Confirmability:* Every synthetic sentence must be confirmable." Here both restrictions are dispensed with. Predicates which are confirmable but not testable are admitted; and generalized sentences are admitted. This is the most liberal of the four requirements. But it suffices to exclude all sentences of a nonempirical nature, e.g., those of transcendental metaphysics, inasmuch as they are not confirmable, even incompletely. Therefore, it seems to Carnap that it suffices as a formulation of the principle of empiricism; in other words, if a scientist chooses any language fulfilling this requirement, no objection can be raised against this choice from the point of view of empiricism.[50]

The main result is, then, that the discussion as to what sentences may be considered meaningful and what sentences meaningless, from the point of view of empiricism, has led, on the one hand, to a more precise definition of and distinction between various empirical languages and so to various concepts of meaning in an empirical sense and, on the other, to the acceptance of the most liberal of the alternatives compatible with empiricism. And this, Carnap thinks, has helped to smooth the way for the development of converging views and approaches to *scientific empiricism* as a movement comprising all allied groups—an ever more scientific philosophy. This aim is closely connected with the idea of a unity of science that has already been mentioned several times but which we shall now carry a little further.

12. Unity of Science and Physicalism

The expression 'unity of science' was introduced into logical empiricism by Neurath. He wanted thereby to mark his opposition to the view that there are different *kinds* of sciences (and, corresponding to them, different kinds of reality or being), such as natural sciences (*Naturwissenschaften*) versus the humanities (*Geisteswissenschaften*), or factual sciences (*Wirklichkeitswissenschaften*) versus normative sciences (*Normwissenschaften*). He also wanted, by the words 'unity of science', to sum up the objective aimed at by logical empiricists, viz., the formation of a science comprising all human knowledge as an epistemologically homogeneous ordered mass of sentences being of the same empiricist nature in principle, from protocol-sentences to the most comprehensive laws for the phenomena of nature and human life.[51] To use a traditional expression, unity of science might also be called "monism free from metaphysics." A first manifestation of this attitude in the Vienna Circle was Carnap's theory of constitution, which Neurath, however, for the above-mentioned (p. 69) reasons found unacceptable. He thought it very important that the unification of the various special sciences into a unity of science should take place through the formation of a universal language of science, i.e., a language the logical syntax of which permitted sentences from the most different special sciences to be combined with one another so as to form a logical context. "The universal language of science becomes a self-evident demand, if it is asked, how can certain singular predictions be derived; e.g., 'the forest fire will soon subside'. In order to do this we need meteorological and botanical sentences and in addition sentences which contain the terms 'man' and 'human behavior'. We must speak of how people react to fire, which social institutions will come into play. Thus, we need sentences from psychology and sociology. They must be able to be placed together with the others in a deduction at whose end is the sentence: 'Therefore, the forest fire will soon subside'."[52] *"We must at times be able to connect all types of laws with one another.* All, whether they be chemical, climatological, or sociological laws, *must be conceived as parts* of one system, viz., unified science."[53] Without this, the practical application of science would be excluded in many domains, and the unity of science therefore forms the basis of the applications of science, depending on the combination of premises from different scientific disciplines into connected chains of inference.

In science as well as in our everyday life we do actually avail ourselves of a kind of "universal slang," whenever we want to reason or to think things over, and the aim of unified science is to make this universal slang homogeneous and universal, eliminating merely metaphysical absurdities. This, however, again raises the question: What language would be best suited for the performance of this task? In his theory of constitution Carnap used, as we know, an egocentric, phenomenological language, thinking that by constitution he would be able to reduce all other concepts to phenomenological basic concepts. But he and Neurath soon agreed that it would be more expedient to use a so-called "physical" or "physicalistic" language or, as it was later called, a "thing-language," by which they understood the language in which we, both in physics and in everyday life, speak of physical things (which again approximately means: material things, in the everyday understanding of that expression). The task then became to formulate the rules of formation and of transformation of such language so that all concepts and sentences can be expressed in it, if necessary, by suitable translations and so that all scientific theories can by means of it be reduced to as few deductive systems as possible, preferably to a single one. "In our discussions in the *Vienna Circle* we have arrived at the opinion that this physical language is the basic language of all science, that it is a universal language comprehending the contents of all other scientific languages. In other words, every sentence of any branch of scientific language is equipollent to some sentence of the physical language, and can therefore be translated into the physical language without changing its content. Dr. Neurath, who has greatly stimulated the considerations which led to this thesis, has proposed to call it the thesis of *physicalism*."[54]

The physical language, Carnap says further, is characteristic, in that it consists of sentences that give in their simplest form a quantitative description of a definite space-time-place (e.g., 'At such and such space-time-point the temperature is so and so many degrees'), or, expressed formally: Sentences that attribute to a certain series of values of space-time-co-ordinates a certain value of a definite physical function. In so far as rules are known for a unique translation of sentences of qualitative characteristics into sentences of quantitative characteristics, there is nothing to prevent the physical language from containing characteristics of the former kind.[55]

The reason for choosing such a language as that of unified science is that it is *intersensual, intersubjective, and universal*. What this means will now be outlined.

That the physical language is *intersensual* means that its sentences can be tested by means of various senses, because actually there is no physical function that can be co-ordinated solely with qualitative characteristics from a single sphere of sense. The characteristic "tone of such and such pitch, timbre, and loudness" may, for instance, be co-ordinated with the following characteristic in the physical language: "Material oscillation of such and such basic frequency with such and such harmonic frequencies with such and such amplitudes," which, by application of certain apparatuses, may be tested by means of the sense of sight or of touch. And, similarly, qualitative characteristics of color may be co-ordinated to physical characteristics of electromagnetic oscillations, which may, for instance, be tested by means of their place in the spectroscope, that may again, by suitable devices, be demonstrated by contact with an indicating needle or by ascertainment of a tone by listening, so that a blind physicist will very well be able to test the qualitative protocol-sentence, 'Here is now green of that and that shade'. It is therefore possible in principle to construct a physical language of such a kind that the qualitative characteristics of the protocol-language depend functionally and uniquely on the distribution of values of physical functions, so that *the physical characteristics may be said to apply intersensually.*[56]

That the physical language is *intersubjective* means that its sentences can be tested by various subjects and thus hold a meaning for all of them. This appears from the fact that a given subject (individual) can observe by means of experiments under what physical conditions various other subjects react by certain qualitative protocol-sentences, e.g., 'I now see green of that and that shade'. Thus a correspondence may be established between every single physical characteristic, on the one hand, and the qualitative characteristics contained in the protocol-sentences of the various subjects, on the other, so that *the physical characteristics may be asserted to apply intersubjectively.*[57]

That the above co-ordinations between physical and qualitative characteristics can be established is no logical necessity but depends on empirical "happy circumstances" connected with "a very general structural feature of experience."[58]

Finally, that the physical language is *universal* means that every scientifically acceptable sentence, whether originating from our everyday language or from a branch of science, can be translated into it. When investigating this view, it is necessary to distinguish between the question of the translatability of protocol-sentences and the question of the translatability of other sentences of the natural and social sciences.

As to the protocol-sentences, the assertion that they are in principle translatable depends on the so-called "logical behaviorism,"[59] which says that sentences concerning mental phenomena (experiences, observations, recollections, emotions, etc.) possess a meaning that can be intersubjectively tested only if they are conceived as sentences concerning the bodily condition and/or behavior of the individual concerned, such as, for example, the condition of his nervous system or his appearance and movements (including also movements of speech).

As regards the remaining sentences belonging to the natural and social sciences, it appears that the translation into the physical language cannot be accomplished solely by explicit definitions but also requires the application of the "reduction" defined by Carnap.[60] This operation has a function similar to that of "constitution" in *Der logische Aufbau der Welt*, but, contrary to constitution, reduction is defined in the formal mode of speech, and the definition is expressed exactly by means of logistic symbols. To go into details would take us too far, but, roughly speaking, it may be said that the content of the definition is that a term 'a' is "reducible" to other terms 'b', 'c', . . . , if it is possible by means of the latter to formulate the characteristics concerning the conditions under which we are going to use the term 'a'. "The simplest method of reducing, in this sense, one concept to another is by definition. If 'a' can be defined by 'b', 'c', . . . , then obviously 'a' is reducible to 'b', 'c'. . . . It can, however, be shown that the method of definition is not the only one but is the simplest special case of reduction. E.g., the concept 'electrical field' is reducible to the concepts 'body,' 'mass,' 'electric charge,' and spatiotemporal determinations. We can, by the use of these concepts, formulate rules for the application of the concept 'electrical field,' viz., describe an experimental test for this concept. On the other hand, we cannot give a definition of 'electrical field' which contains only those concepts. Therefore, we must distinguish the broader concept 'reducibility' from the narrower concept 'definability.' "[61]

While reduction by definition cannot be carried through even with regard to the concepts of physics, nothing seems to prevent the reduction of the total number of concepts of the natural and social sciences to the physical language, if reduction is taken in its wider and more liberal sense, and this procedure is therefore suggested for unified science. The crucial points, where special difficulties might be expected to arise, concern the translations of biological, psychological, and sociological sentences into the physical language. As is well known, the material mode of speech has often led us to conceive the objects of those sciences as different in principle and (in a not specified sense) mutually irreducible. But the translation into the formal mode of speech of the sentences about these sciences shows that a reduction of their concepts to the physical language is possible in principle, and that, accordingly, the advantages attached to the realization of the idea of the unity of science are within reach, although to carry it out in detail would, of course, require both much more special investigation and a greatly extended co-operation among the investigators of the special sciences, mutually, and between them and logicians. In order to convey an idea of the view of the logical empiricists, their attitude to the three crucial points mentioned should be dealt with briefly.

In regard to biological sentences, logical empiricists think that the possibility of their translation into the physical language is evident, considering that all biological concepts capable of being empirically tested concern conditions and processes in bodies that may be characterized by space-time-co-ordinates. The vitalistic concepts, such as "entelechy," etc., that are incapable of being tested must, of course, be dropped, while the analysis of concepts such as "whole" and "purposiveness" has not as yet been performed in detail but will hardly give rise to difficulties in principle.

As regards the translatability of psychological sentences, logical behaviorism is invoked. If this is tenable, the translatability in principle of psychological sentences into the physical language is evident. And, having once gone so far, there seems no possibility of insurmountable difficulties in connection with the translation of sociological sentences, which describe the relation of persons and other organisms to one another and to their surroundings.

In addition to these considerations concerning general principles, logical empiricists also, in support of the idea of a unity of science, refer to the many border sciences growing up in an increasing number and bearing witness to formerly unheeded cross-connections between the traditional branches of science, such as biophysics, biochemistry, psychophysiology, social psychology, etc.; and the result of their deliberations is that they think themselves entitled to assert that "the concepts of the thing-language provide a common basis to which all concepts of all the parts of science can be reduced"[62]—only, of course, in the above-mentioned sense of "reduction."

This result only justifies a continuation of the work of realizing the idea of the unity of science. A road has been opened for a detailed analysis of the concepts of the individual sciences for the purpose of showing how the sentences of every one of them may be reduced to the thing-language. But the analysis itself is, of course, a gigantic piece of work that can be performed only by the co-operation of logicians and the specialists within the various special sciences. Such co-operation has indeed also been eagerly sought by logical empiricists from the early days of the Vienna Circle, and the ever increasing number of special scientists participating in the congresses is impressive evidence of the fact that this need for co-operation is widely felt. Its most conspicuous expression has been, perhaps, in the *International Encyclopedia of Unified Science*, where scientists of the special sciences and philosophers work together in harmony, although they are completely free to express varying opinions on questions of doubt. Strictly speaking, the thesis of physicalism cannot be considered proved until the reduction to the thing-language of the total number of the concepts of the natural and social sciences is made, which means, of course, never. But this in no way makes the work on the creation of an ever greater connection within the sphere of sciences superfluous, let alone useless. And should it appear that concepts actually exist which cannot be reduced to the thing-language—well, then, that does not make the idea of unity less valuable but merely shows that it is necessary to choose another language than the thing-language as the language of unity, which may very well be possible, although care should be taken, of course, that a reasonable meaning can always be attached to the sentences of any such language.[63]

As regards the question of the reduction of scientific theories to a few or even a single deductive system, the prospects are, in the opinion of logical empiricists, much darker than where the question of the reduction of concepts to the physical thing-language is concerned. Not even all physical laws can at present be included in a single deductive theory, and the prospects for a derivation of biological from physical laws—let alone a derivation of psychological or sociological laws from the physical plus the biological laws—are distant, although not hopeless. Efforts are being made to create more comprehensive syntheses, and no limits can be set beforehand to these endeavors. Yet, in spite of the great advantage of a unity of laws, its importance is not so fundamental as that of the unity of language,[64] which is more easily achieved.

13. Present Tendencies and Tasks

In this exposition of the development of logical empiricism I have kept largely to the main lines of development, and I hope that I have succeeded in making them clear. I have had to leave completely out of consideration a great many penetrating individual analyses, some of which have been the conditions and others the fruits of this development. So far logical-mathematical and physical concepts, theories, and methods have been treated, whereas biological, psychological, and sociological subjects, as well as concepts and theories of value, have been only occasionally touched upon. But the very idea of a unity of science implies that all spheres of knowledge should be treated, and the predilection for the exact sciences is a defect, against which the gradually growing connection with the views developed within pragmatism should now serve as a useful remedy. As yet, we are in these domains at the beginner's stage, which is to some extent due to the relative backwardness of these sociohumanistic sciences. However, from the co-operation with pragmatists and operationalists especially interested in biology, psychology, and sociology results may be expected which are necessary in order to create a proper balance of things. At the Harvard congress of 1939 this tendency made itself plainly felt and also came to expression in Morris' paper, "Semiotic, the Sociohumanistic Sciences, and the Unity of Science," in which he showed that the so far neglected spheres of knowledge can, in principle, be incorporated into unified science via a comprehensive theory of signs, or semiotic, a point which he later developed in his *Signs, Language, and Behavior* (1946). The same tendency was also pronounced in Joergensen's paper at the Harvard congress, "Empiricism and Unity of Science," in which especially the incorporation of the formal sciences into unified science was sketched and an attempt made to establish this contact through psychology; this conception was later expounded in his *Psykologi paa biologisk Grundlag* ("Psychology Based on Biology") (1941–45). Since the precise apparatus of concepts and the refined methods which have resulted from the work with the analysis of the exact sciences have proved highly useful in the further realization of the program of the unity of science, it is possible that the development in this direction may proceed more quickly than might have been expected, in view of the relatively great complication of these spheres. Prospects seem bright for the further development of logical empiricism, which has had the good luck to be stimulated by the metaphysical verbosity re-emerging in the wake of the last war, in almost the same way as the Vienna school and its predecessors were in their day stimulated by the unverifiable nebulous speaking of speculative metaphysicians.

Another tendency came to expression at the Harvard congress, namely, an increasing interest in semantics, which had, in particular, been developed by the Lwow-Warsaw school but which, so far, in the works of the logical empiricists had been overshadowed by logical syntax. While syntax is exclusively concerned with purely formal relations between linguistic expressions *qua* mere figures, semantics treats of the relations between the expressions of a given language and their "designata," i.e., that which they designate. In his paper, "Science and Analysis of Language," Carnap stressed the great significance of semantics and characterized as semantical several main concepts which he had formerly regarded as syntactical. This applies, for example, to concepts like "consequence," "analytic," "contradictory," and others, all of which are based on the important semantical concept of truth. As to the connection between them, Carnap said: "I have explained the semantical analysis of a language as exhibiting the relation of designation. We might equally well regard it as exhibiting the truth-conditions of the sentences of the language in question. This is merely a different formulation of the aim of semantics. Suppose a sentence of the simplest form is given, consisting of a proper name combined with a one-place predicate (e.g. 'Switzerland is small'); if, now, we know which object is designated by the name and which property is designated by the predicate then we also know the truth-condition of the sentence: it is true if the object designated by the name has the property designated by the predicate. Thus the concept of *truth* turns out to be one of the fundamental concepts of semantics. We may say that the result of a semantical analysis of a sentence is the understanding of the sentence. To understand a sentence is to know what is designated by the terms occurring in the sentence and, hence, to know under what conditions it will be true. But the understanding of a sentence does not suffice, in general, for knowing whether those conditions are fulfilled, in other words, whether the sentence is true or not. But sometimes there is such a relation between two sentences that a semantical analysis of them, in other words, the understanding of the sentences, suffices to show that if the first sentence is true the second must also be true. In this case the second is called a *logical consequence* of the first. This concept, the basic concept of the theory of logical deduction and thereby of logic itself, is thus based upon a certain relation between truth-conditions, and hence is a semantical concept. The same holds for other logical concepts which are often applied in the logical analysis of science, e.g. logically true (analytic), logically false (contradictory), logically indeterminate or factual (synthetic, neither logically true nor logically false), logically compatible, etc."[65] In consequence of the above view, Carnap later, in his *Introduction to Semantics* (1943), replaced his earlier syntactical definitions of the concepts mentioned by semantical definitions and also found it necessary, in general, to supplement many of the former discussions and analyses by corresponding semantical ones. They were not incorrect, to be sure, but they were incomplete. Perhaps the awakening interest in the pragmatic views developed by Morris and others will show that semantical analyses are not exhaustive either; but this question belongs to the future.

To characterize in brief the value of the contribution of logical empiricism to the development of human knowledge can best be done, I believe, by emphasizing that it has led to the appearance of entirely new points of view as regards philosophical problems. These must today be posed in a way that differs in principle from the ones hitherto used, and their treatment requires much more exactness than has been exercised heretofore. The very fact that we have grown accustomed to ask for the *meaning* of words and sentences and have found useful criteria has intensified our criticism of statements made by ourselves and by others and has thus furthered the critical attitude which, combined with inventiveness and imagination, is the basic condition for a sensible approach to the practical problems of our day and to the promotion of scientific investigation. To return to past ways of thinking would be like ignoring the quantum theory in physics. Or, in other words, it is, as matters stand, impracticable. And to have made a contribution which it is impossible to ignore if scientific investigation is to proceed is presumably the utmost that may be expected from the pursuers of science. But this expectation the pioneers of logical empiricism have already fulfilled. And if today the still unsolved problems within the sphere of philosophy can be formulated and treated with a precision and clarity formerly unknown, the merit is theirs. They have not created a new philosophical system, which, indeed, would have been contrary to their highest intentions, but they have paved the way for a new and fruitful manner of philosophizing.

Notes and Bibliography

Chapter I

1. See Postscript, bringing this material up to date.

2. H. Feigl, "Logical Empiricism," in *Twentieth Century Philosophy*, ed. Dagobert D. Runes (New York, 1947), pp. 406–8. Compare Otto Neurath, *Le Développement du cercle de Vienne et l'avenir de l'empirisme logique* (Paris, 1935), chap. v, where he attempts to show the reason why the movement originated just in Vienna, where liberalistic and empiricist trends had made themselves felt for several decades, which had not been the case in Germany.

3. *Wissenschaftliche Weltauffassung*, pp. 16–17.

4. Neurath, *Le Développement du cercle de Vienne*, p. 58.

5. See, e.g., P. Frank, "Logisierender Empirismus in der Philosophie der U.S.S.R.," *Actes du congrès international de philosophie scientifiques, Sorbonne, Paris, 1935* (Paris, 1936), VIII, 68–76.

6. As a curiosity it may be noted that Comte is not mentioned at all in Russell's large *A History of Western Philosophy* (London, 1946). Even Ernst Mach is not mentioned.

7. Cf. Jean Nicod, "Les Tendences philosophiques de M. Bertrand Russell," *Revue de mét. et de mor.*, XXIX (1922), 77.

8. Concerning Mach's relation to logical empiricism see R. von Mises, "Ernst Mach und die empiristische Wissenschaftsauffassung," *Einheitswissenschaft* ("Library of Unified Science," No. 7 ['s Gravenhage, 1938]).

9. B. Russell, *Our Knowledge of the External World as a Field for Scientific Method in Philosophy* (Chicago, 1914), chap. ii.

10. *Ibid.*

11. B. Russell, "Logical Atomism," *Contemporary British Philosophy: Personal Statements, First Series* (London and New York, 1924), p. 363.

12. Russell, *Our Knowledge*, p. 112.

13. *Ibid.*, p. 111.

14. *Ibid.*, p. 78.

15. *Ibid.*, p. 89.

16. *Ibid.*, pp. 111–12.

17. G. E. Moore, *Principia ethica* (Cambridge, 1903), p. ix.

18. See, e.g., R. B. Braithwaite, "Philosophy", in *Cambridge University Studies*, VII (1933), pp. 1–32.

19. Russell's Introduction to Wittgenstein, *Tractatus* (London, 1922), p. 8.

20. H. M. Sheffer, "A Set of Five Independent Postulates for Boolean Algebras, with Application to Logical Constants," *Trans. Amer. Math. Soc.*, XIV (1913), 488–89.

21. Cf. Russell's Introduction to *Tractatus*, pp. 13–15.

22. Carnap, *Scheinprobleme*, pp. 27–29.

23. Carnap, *Der logische Aufbau der Welt*, p. 2.

24. *Ibid.*, p. 47.

25. *Ibid.*, pp. 57–58.

26. *Ibid.*, p. 65.

27. *Ibid.*, p. 74.

Notes and Bibliography

28. *Ibid.*, p. 139.

29. *Ibid.*, p. 79.

30. *Ibid.*, p. 80.

31. *Ibid.*, p. 86.

32. *Ibid.*, p. 87.

33. *Ibid.*, p. 92.

34. *Ibid.*, pp. 93–104.

35. *Ibid.*, p. 102.

36. *Ibid.*, pp. 109–10.

37. *Ibid.*, p. 133.

38. *Ibid.*, p. 23.

39. *Ibid.*, p. 169.

40. *Ibid.*, p. 176.

41. *Ibid.*, pp. 186–87.

42. *Ibid.*, p. 202.

43. *Ibid.*, p. 204.

44. *Ibid.*

45. *Ibid.*, pp. 245–55.

46. A brief survey of the first stages of this internal criticism will be found in A. Petzäll, *Logistischer Positivismus* ("Göteborgs Högskolas Årsskrift," Vol. XXXVII Göteborg, [1931]). Incidentally, it may be noted that the first thoroughgoing criticism of Carnap's *Der logische Aufbau der Welt* was advanced by another Scandinavian philosopher, Eino Kaila, who, like Petzäll, had studied in Vienna, in his penetrating essay, *Der logische Positivismus: Eine kritische Studie* (Turku, 1930). Kaila later gave valuable contributions to certain parts of the theory of constitution in his *Das System der Wirklichkeitsbegriffe* (Helsingfors, 1936) and his *Den mänskliga Kunskapen* ("Human Knowledge") (Helsingfors, 1939). A comprehensive critical study which also considers the later development of the movement is J. R. Weinberg's *An Examination of Logical Positivism* (London, 1936).

Chapter II

1. M. Schlick, "The Future of Philosophy," *Seventh International Congress of Philosophy, Oxford, 1930* (Oxford, 1931), p. 112. A more detailed discussion under the same title, "The Future of Philosophy," was published in *Publications in Philosophy*, ed. P. A. Schilpp, Vol. I (College of the Pacific, 1932). This lecture was reprinted in *Gesammelte Aufsätze* (Vienna, 1938) and in *Basic Problems of Philosophy*, ed. D. J. Bronstein *et al.* (New York, 1947).

2. "The Future of Philosophy," p. 115.

3. *Ibid.*, p. 116.

4. See *Erkenntnis* I (1930), 72.

5. H. Reichenbach, *Relativitätstheorie und Erkenntnis apriori* (Berlin, 1920), p. 71.

6. H. Reichenbach, "Logistic Empiricism in Germany and the Present State of Its Problems," *Journal of Philosophy*, XXXIII (1936), 114.

7. Reichenbach, *Relativitätstheorie und Erkenntnis apriori*, p. 74.

8. Reichenbach, *Philosophie der Raum-Zeit-Lehre*, p. 45.

9. *Ibid.*, pp. 205–6.

10. Reichenbach, *Ziele und Wege der heutigen Naturphilosophie* (Leipzig, 1931), pp. 38–39.

11. Reichenbach, *Wahrscheinlichkeitslehre* (Leiden, 1935), p. 381.

12. *Ibid.*, p. 387.

13. Reichenbach, "Logistic Empiricism," p. 157; cf. also his *Experience and Prediction*, p. 363.

14. See Reichenbach, *Wahrscheinlichkeitslehre*, p. 305, and his *Experience and Prediction*, p. 363.

15. Reichenbach, "Logistic Empiricism," pp. 158–59.

16. Cf. Ajdukiewicz, "Der logistische Antiirrationalismus in Polen," *Erkenntnis*, V, 151; and Rose Rand, "Kotarbinski's Philosophie auf Grund seines Hauptwerkes: 'Elemente der Erkenntnistheorie, der Logik und der Methodologie der Wissenschaften,'" *Erkenntnis*, VII, 92. See also Z. Jordan's book (Postscript).

17. See, e.g., C. Morris, "Some Aspects of Recent American Scientific Philosophy," *Erkenntnis*, V, 142.

18. C. S. Peirce, "How To Make Our Ideas Clear," *Popular Science Monthly*, January, 1878, here quoted from Peirce, *Chance, Love, and Logic: Philosophical Essays* (London, 1923), p. 45.

19. P. W. Bridgman, *The Logic of Modern Physics* (New York, 1927), pp. 5–7; see also two articles by Herbert Feigl on operationism and explanation in *Psychological Review*, LII, 195; reprinted in *Readings in Philosophical Analysis* (see Postscript).

20. C. Morris, "The Concept of Meaning in Pragmatism and Logical Positivism," *Actes du huitième congrès international de philosophie à Prague, 2–7 septembre, 1934* (Prague, 1936), p. 133.

21. C. Morris, *Logical Positivism, Pragmatism, and Scientific Empiricism* (Paris, 1937), p. 65. Morris has recently given a comprehensive exposition of his semiotic in *Signs, Language, and Behavior* (New York, 1040).

22. See, e.g., K. Marc-Wogau's article, "Uppsala Filosofien och den logiska Empirismen," *Ord och Bild* (1944), p. 30, where similarities and differences between the two movements have been clearly stated.

23. In *Philosophy of Science*, I (1934), 5.

24. Published in a revised and enlarged English translation entitled *The Logical Syntax of Language* (1936). In his *Die Aufgabe der Wissenshaftslogik* (in the collection "Einheitswissenschaft," No. 3 [1934]) and in his London lectures, *Philosophy and Logical Syntax* (London, 1935), Carnap has given more popular expositions of his theory.

25. Carnap, *Logical Syntax of Language* (London, 1937), pp. 51–52.

26. Carnap, *Philosophy and Logical Syntax*, pp. 47–49.

27. *Ibid.*, p. 56.

28. This point of view Carnap had already advanced in his article, "Die physikalische Sprache als Universalsprache der Wissenschaft," *Erkenntnis*, II (1931), 432.

29. Carnap, *Philosophy and Logical Syntax*, pp. 81–82.

30. *Ibid.*, pp. 80–81.

31. O. Neurath, "Soziologie im Physikalismus," *Erkenntnis*, II (1931), 403; cf. also O. Neurath, "Physikalismus," *Scientia*, 1931, p. 299.

32. M. Schlick, "Über das Fundament der Erkenntnis," *Erkenntnis*, IV (1933), 96–97.

33. *Ibid.*, p. 98.

34. O. Neurath, "Radikaler Physikalismus und 'wirkliche Welt,'" *Erkenntnis*, IV (1933), 361.

35. *Ibid.*, p. 356.   36. *Ibid.*, p. 352.

37. O. Neurath, "Protokollsätze," *Erkenntnis*, III (1932), 206.

38. In *Analysis*, II (1935), 49.

39. *Ibid.*, p. 93.

40. K. Popper, *Logik der Forschung* (Vienna, 1935), p. 9.

41. M. Schlick, "Die Kausalität in der gegenwärtigen Physik," *Naturwissenschaften*, XIX (1931), 156.

Notes and Bibliography

42. Popper, *Logik der Forschung*, p. 13.

43. Published in *Philosophy of Science*, III (1936), 419, and IV (1937), 1.

44. R. Carnap, "Wahrheit und Bewährung," *Actes du congrès international de philosophie scientifique, Paris, 1935* (Paris, 1936), IV, 19.

45. *Philosophy of Science*, III, 20–21.

46. This question was discussed later in detail by C. G. Hempel in his "A Purely Syntactical Definition of Confirmation," *Journal of Symbolic Logic*, Vol. VIII (1943), and in "Studies in the Logic of Confirmation," *Mind*, LIV (1945), 1 and 97.

47. *Philosophy of Science*, IV, 33.

48. *Ibid.*, p. 34.

49. *Ibid.*

50. *Ibid.*, pp. 34–35. As to the view here mentioned, see also C. G. Hempel, "Le Problème de la vérité," *Theoria*, 1937, p. 206.

51. See, e.g., O. Neurath, *Empirische Soziologie: Der wissenschaftliche Gehalt der Geschichte und Nationalökonomie* (Vienna, 1931), p. 2.

52. O. Neurath, *Einheitswissenschaft und Psychologie* (Vienna, 1933), p. 7.

53. O. Neurath, "Soziologie im Physikalismus," *Erkenntnis*, II (1931), 395.

54. R. Carnap, *Philosophy and Logical Syntax*, p. 89.

55. R. Carnap, "Die physikalische Sprache als Universalsprache der Wissenschaft," *Erkenntnis*, II (1931), 441–42.

56. *Ibid.*, p. 445.

57. *Ibid.*, p. 447.

58. *Ibid.*

59. See, e.g., C. G. Hempel, "Analyse logique de la psychologie," *Revue de synthèse*, X (1935), 27; and R. Carnap, "Les Concepts psychologiques et les concepts physiques sont-ils foncièrement différentes?" *Revue de synthèse*, X (1935), 43.

60. R. Carnap, "Testability and Meaning," *Philosophy of Science*, III, 434.

61. Carnap, "Einheit der Wissenschaft durch Einheit der Sprache," *Travaux du IX⁰ congrès international de philosophie* (Paris, 1937), IV, 54. Cf. Carnap, "Ueber die Einheitssprache der Wissenschaft: Logische Bemerkungen zum Projekt einer Enzyklopädie," *Actes du congrès international de philosophie scientifique* (Paris, 1936), II, 60.

62. Carnap, "Einheit der Wissenschaft," p. 57.

63. I could imagine, for instance, that one might go so far as to give up intersubjectivity and accordingly admit sentences as meaningful, if only they are introspectively testable (and so not mere sound-complexes with no designations) or, at any rate, introspective sentences that agree to such an extent as to fulfil the requirements generally made by psychologists for the admittance of their universal validity in psychology. In case a criterion of meaning as liberal as this is accepted, logical behaviorism will no longer be a necessary condition of such extended unity of science but merely a special means of testing, side by side with introspection. However, actual metaphysical sentences of untestable entities would be excluded as meaningless.

64. Cf. R. Carnap, *Logical Foundations of the Unity of Science*, in *Encyclopedia of Unified Science*, I, No. 1 (Chicago, 1938), 60–62.

65. Here quoted from a separate print distributed at the congress. A similar reaction to the prevalent formal-syntactical view came simultaneously to expression in J. Joergensen's "Reflexions on Logic and Language. I. Languages, Games, and Empiricism; II. Semantical Logic," *Journal of Unified Science (Erkenntnis)*, VIII (1939), 218.

Postscript

By Norman M. Martin

World War II caused considerable disturbance in the movement of logical empiricism. Most of the European philosophers survived, and many of them left the Continent for Great Britain or the United States. Hosiasson and Lindenbaum died in Poland; Kurt Grelling and Karl Reach were deported by the Nazis and died or were killed. The *Journal of Unified Science* and the "Library of Unified Science" were discontinued because of the war. The work on the *International Encyclopedia of Unified Science* was hampered, although a number of monographs were issued (see chap. ii, part 1).

The war did not, however, put an end to the work of the logical empiricists. On the contrary, this work continued along several lines. The Sixth International Congress for the Unity of Science was held at the University of Chicago, September 2–6, 1941. Some of the main topics were the unification of science, the theory of signs, psychology, and valuation. Since then no congresses have been held.

Considerable progress has been made in semantics. Especially important here are the contributions of Carnap. His *Introduction to Semantics* (Cambridge: Harvard University Press, 1942) presents the problems involved in the construction of semantical systems, especially with the construction of L-concepts, i.e., concepts which are applicable on merely logical reasons as opposed to factual reasons, and with the relations between syntax and semantics. He there explains in detail how he would modify the views expressed in his *Logical Syntax of Language*. Further attention to the relation between semantics and syntax is paid in Carnap's *Formalization of Logic* (Cambridge: Harvard University Press, 1943). By "formalization" is meant the construction of a syntactical concept which applies whenever a given semantical concept applies in any semantical system which is a true interpretation of the constructed calculus. For example,

C-implication (derivability) in logical syntax is intended as a formalization of L-implication. The problem of the book is whether the calculi common today are full formalizations of logic and, if not, whether such a formalization can be made. Carnap shows that the usual propositional calculus is not a full formalization of propositional logic but that, with the introduction of a new type of syntactical concept called "junctives," a full formalization can be achieved. Similar results hold for functional logic.

In *Meaning and Necessity* (Chicago: University of Chicago Press, 1947) Carnap suggests the substitution of the method of extension and intension for the method of the name-relation, which had dominated earlier semantical discussion. By this method, instead of considering an expression as the name of an entity, it would be considered to have an intension and an extension; e.g., the predicate 'red' has the property of being red as its intension and the class of red things as its extension. Carnap proposes to use the concepts of intension and extension, which occurred now and again in the old logic, as key concepts in semantical analysis. He discusses the possibility of an adequate extensional metalanguage for semantics and finds it, in general, possible, although there are some doubtful features. He also outlines a system of modal logic which he constructs in greater detail in "Modalities and Quantification," *Journal of Symbolic Logic*, XI (1946), 33–64.

Several interesting contributions to semantic theory are contained in the "Symposium on Meaning and Truth" which appeared in Volumes IV (1944) and V (1945) of *Philosophy and Phenomenological Research*. C. I. Lewis, in "Modes of Meaning" (*ibid.*, Vol. IV), gives an analysis of language similar in many respects to the intension-extension distinction made by Carnap. He distinguishes (as terms): denotation—the class of all actual things to which a term applies; comprehension—the class of all consistently thinkable things to which a term applies; connotation—which is identified with a correct definition of the term; and signification—the comprehensive character such that everything that has that character is correctly namable by the term.

Analogous distinctions are made for sentences. G. Watts Cunningham, in "On the Linguistic Meaning-Situation" (*ibid.*, Vol. IV), attempts to specify the limits of conventionalism in semantics by asserting that, while the words and rules of syntax of a language are conventional, the syntactical structure is determined by the referent. Felix Kaufmann, in "Verification, Meaning, and Truth" (*ibid.*, Vol. IV), attempts to define truth in terms of agreement with the rules of scientific procedure—a position not unlike that of Neurath. C. J. Ducasse, in "Propositions, Truth, and the Ultimate Criterion of Truth" (*ibid.*, Vol. IV), defends the view that ultimate "undisbelievability" is the criterion of truth. Alfred Tarski, in "The Semantic Conception of Truth" (*ibid.*, Vol. IV), presents in English the main features of the definition of truth which he had presented earlier in Polish and German; he clarifies the nature of this concept and defends his views against his critics. Norman Dalkey, in "The Limits of Meaning" (*ibid.*, Vol. IV), gives an analysis of vagueness, pointing out three elements which he terms "confusion," "obscurity," and "incomplete determination." These views were discussed by the symposiasts and by Ernest Nagel, who came out strongly against Ducasse's formulations, in later issues of the journal.

Another significant line of work, which was pursued throughout the war years, was the analysis of science. A collection of articles by Philipp Frank, dating from 1908 to 1938, which dealt with the philosophy of physics was published under the name *Between Physics and Philosophy* (Cambridge: Harvard University Press, 1941). Felix Kaufmann presented his theory of scientific procedure in *Methodology of the Social Sciences* (New York: Oxford University Press, 1944). He emphasizes particularly the reliance of scientific procedure on rules (often implicit) of procedure. Thus, for him, the reversibility of the decision to accept a proposition into the body of knowledge (the principle of permanent control) and the necessity of having grounds for the acceptance of a proposition are extremely important. Rules of scientific procedure may in his opinion be changed, but only in connection with "rules of higher order." In line with this approach, Kaufmann discusses methodological issues, first of empirical science in general, and then, in particular, of problems in social science, such as value-statements, behaviorism, and the nature of social law.

Another important work is Hans Reichenbach's *Philosophical Foundations of Quantum Mechanics*, in which he discusses the mathematics of quantum mechanics and the problems of its interpretation, suggesting that a three-valued logic is more suitable for this purpose than the usual two-valued logic. Quantum mechanics can be formulated in one of three ways, in a wave language, a corpuscle language, or a neutral (three-valued) language. In the first two, sentences expressing causal anomalies appear. These do not appear in the neutral language; however, sentences about interphenomena do appear when this language is used.

In *Elements of Symbolic Logic* (New York: Macmillan Co., 1947) Reichenbach attempts to characterize the logic of scientific laws. He does this with the help of the concept of "original nomological statement," which he defines as "an all-statement that is demonstrably true, fully exhaustive, and universal." Then he is able to describe the common character of all laws. In the same book he also gives an analysis of grammar from the standpoint of modern logic.

An interesting contribution to the logical analysis of science is "Studies in the Logic of Explanation," by Carl G. Hempel and Paul Oppenheim, in *Philosophy of Science*, XV (1948), 135–75. Hempel and Oppenheim attempt to examine explanation by looking at the conditions that the explanans must fulfil. The principal requirements are: the explanandum must be a logical consequence of the explanans; the explanans must contain general laws, and these must actually be required in the derivation of the explanandum; the explanans must be capable, at least in principle, of test by experiment or observation, and the sentences constituting the explanans must be true. The authors hold that these criteria are general throughout science. In this connection they discuss the concept of "emergence," concluding that it must be purged of its connotations of absolute unpredictability. In line with these views they construct a precise logical theory of explanation.

A great deal of discussion on the philosophy of probability has occurred. In the "Symposium on Probability" which took place in *Philosophy and Phenomenological Research*, Volumes V (1945) and VI (1946), Donald Williams defends the Laplacean conception, which was attacked from a frequency point of view by Reichenbach, von Mises, and Margenau. Carnap, in "The Two Concepts of Probability" (*ibid.*, Vol. V [1945], 513–32), defends the view that there are actually two distinct concepts used under the name of "probability," both of which have a right to scientific treatment. The first of these concepts is sometimes also called "degree of confirmation," the second, "relative frequency in the long run." Carnap then illustrates at length the differences in logical nature between the two concepts. The first of these concepts is a semantical one dealing with relations between sentences; the second is an empirical concept. A basic sentence of the first is true by logic alone and one of the second by virtue of the facts. In "On Inductive Logic," *Philosophy of Science*, XII (1945), 72–97, Carnap elaborated his system of probability in the sense of degree of confirmation. The exposition of his system of inductive logic will constitute the bulk of his forthcoming two-volume work, *Probability and Induction*. Felix Kaufmann held, in "Scientific Procedure and Probability," in *Philosophy and Phenomenological Research*, VI (1945), 47–66, that degree of confirmation should be defined in terms of the process of accepting propositions into the body of accepted knowledge. For this reason he wants to distinguish sharply between the confirmation of a proposition not yet accepted and the corroboration of one already accepted. An alternative definition of degree of confirmation to that offered by Carnap was presented by Hempel and Oppenheim in "A Definition of 'Degree of Confirmation,' " *Philosophy of Science*, XII (1945), 98–115, and by Olaf Helmer and Oppenheim in "A Syntactical Definition of Probability and Degree of Confirmation," *Journal of Symbolic Logic*, X (1945), 25–60. This definition is of particular interest, since, when so defined, the degree of confirmation function is not a probability function, i.e., it does not have all the mathematical properties commonly associated with probability in mathematical theory. In the discussions centering around the symposium on probability, Nagel and Bergmann participated actively.

In addition to the above-mentioned works on more or less specific topics, several works of a more general nature on the theory of signs and theory of value were written by logical empiricists. Russell wrote *An Inquiry into Meaning and Truth* (New York: W. W. Norton & Co., 1940), in which he defends a causal theory of language. He holds the view that the proper individuals of an epistemologically correct language are universals. He maintains the necessity of basic propositions, i.e., propositions which are caused (and justified) by perception and which are known to be true. He defends the correspondence theory of truth against Dewey's "warranted assertibility" and similar opinions. Russell also published *A History of Western Philosophy and Its Connections with Political and Social Circumstances* (New York: Simon & Schuster, 1945), in which he attempts to analyze the major philosophers from the standpoint of the philosophy of logical analysis. In addition, Russell wrote *Human Knowledge: Its Scope and Limits* (New York: Simon & Schuster, 1948), in which he deals with problems of epistemology, semiotic, and the philosophy of science. For the first time he deals with the problem of probability; he holds that scientific inference needs some statement of the inductive principle which would be a synthetic statement but could not be established by any argument from experience. He concludes from his general study of knowledge that empiricism is not an adequate theory of knowledge, although less inadequate than previous theories. He also holds that these inadequacies can be discovered by adherence to the doctrine that "all human knowledge is uncertain, inexact and partial."

Charles Morris wrote *Paths of Life* (New York: Harper & Bros., 1942), in which he analyzes the principal patterns of value-preferences and suggests, as a possible means of uniting them in dynamic interaction, one which involves features of all of them. *The Open Self* (New York: Prentice-Hall, 1948) continues his empirical study of value-patterns. In *Signs, Language, and Behavior* (New York: Prentice-Hall, 1946) Morris analyzes meaning-phenomena at length. He distinguishes four modes of signifying: the designative (e.g., "the coin is round"), the appraisive (e.g., "the coin is good"), the prescriptive (e.g., "Come here"), and the formative (e.g., "the coin is a coin"). In addition, four uses of language (informative, valuative, incitive, and systemic) are distinguished. On the basis of these distinctions Morris classifies types of discourse. His point of departure is behavioral (more in the sense of Tolman and Mead than of Watson), and one of his principal results is the formulation of the theory of signs, or semiotic, in behavioral terms. He considers at length the importance and role of signs in individual and social life.

Another important contribution to the theory of meaning is C. I. Lewis' *Analysis of Knowledge and Valuation* (La Salle, Ill.: Open Court Publishing Co., 1946). Lewis begins with a general theory of meaning derived from Peirce, together with the distinction between empirical and analytic statements: the analytic ones are those which relate to meanings alone. Empirical sentences are of three types: first, expressive statements, which express an experience directly and which are, therefore, indubitable to the one who utters them, although they may be false in the case of a lying report—they are thus much like Schlick's substantiations; second, terminating judgments, which make predictions concerning experience specific as to time and place; and, finally, nonterminating judgments, which make predictions concerning experience general as to time and place. Lewis analyzes all knowledge into these types of empirical and analytic sentences. He also presents an analysis of value-sentences so that they are a species of empirical sentence.

Another study concerning the nature of valuation is Charles L. Stevenson's *Ethics and Language* (New Haven: Yale University Press, 1944). Stevenson attempts to distinguish between differences in belief and differences in attitude; valuational statements are analyzed into cognitive and prescriptive components (e.g., 'this is good' is interpreted as 'I approve of this, do so likewise'), and it is maintained that ethical differences are ultimately differences in attitude rather than in belief.

Within the "Library of Living Philosophers," edited by Paul A. Schilpp, two volumes were published under the titles of *The Philosophy of G. E. Moore* (Evanston: Northwestern University, 1942) and *The Philosophy of Bertrand Russell* (Evanston: Northwestern University, 1944). Each of these volumes contains a series of descriptive and critical essays by several authors, together with a reply by the philosopher concerned, and a complete bibliography. Among the contributors are C. D. Broad, C. L. Stevenson, Paul Marhenke, C. M. Langford, John Wisdom, Susan Stebbing, Hans Reichenbach, Kurt Gödel, Max Black, and Ernest Nagel.

An excellent summary of the work done by the Polish groups is presented in *The Development of Mathematical Logic and Logical Positivism in Poland between the Two Wars*, by Z. Jordan (New York: Oxford University Press, 1945). A good summary of the position of logical empiricism, including a selected bibliography of empiricist publications, can be found in Herbert Feigl's article on "Logical Empiricism," in *Twentieth Century Philosophy: Living Schools of Thought*, edited by Dagobert D. Runes (New York: Philosophical Library, 1943). This article and many others by writers of the logical-empiricist movement are reprinted in *Readings in Philosophical Analysis*, edited by Herbert Feigl and Wilfrid Sellars (New York: Appleton-Century-Crofts, 1949). This volume contains sections on semantics, confirmability, logic and mathematics, the a priori, induction and probability, logical analysis of philosophy, philosophy of science and ethics, from viewpoints allied to logical empiricism. Among the authors included, in addition to the editors, are Quine, Tarski, Frege, Russell, Carnap, Lewis, Schlick, Ajdukiewicz, Nagel, Waismann, Hempel, Broad, Ducasse, Reichenbach, and Stevenson, as well as a number of other empiricist philosophers.

The "Discussion on the Unity of Science," in which, among others, Neurath, Morris, and Horace Kallen participated, appeared in *Philosophy and Phenomenological Research*, Volume VI. In 1946, *Synthèse*, an international journal published in Holland, resumed the publication of its "Unity of Science Forum," which had been edited by Neurath until his death in 1945. *Analysis*, which represents, largely, the British analytic philosophers, has also resumed publication.

The movement of logical empiricism, having developed during the war even under unfavorable conditions, is now further expanding its activities.

EDITORS' NOTE: Since the Postscript written by Norman M. Martin early in 1949 a number of developments deserve notice. Among recent publications relevant to the field of this monograph, the following books may be mentioned: M. Black, *Language and Philosophy* (Ithaca: Cornell University Press, 1949); R. Carnap, *Logical Foundations of Probability* (Chicago: University of Chicago Press, 1950)—this is the first volume of the two-volume work, *Probability and Induction;* P. Frank, *Relativity—a Richer Truth* (Boston: Beacon Press, 1950); P. Frank, *Modern Science and Its Philosophy* (Cambridge: Harvard University Press, 1949)—this is an expanded version of his former work, *Between Physics and Philosophy;* A. Pap, *Elements of Analytic Philosophy* (New York: Macmillan Co., 1949); H. Reichenbach, *Theory of Probability* (Berkeley: University of California Press, 1949); P. Schilpp (ed.), *Albert Einstein: Philosopher-Scientist* (Evanston, Ill.: Library of Living Philosophers, 1949). A new journal, *Philosophical Studies*, edited by H. Feigl and W. Sellars, began publication in 1949 (Minneapolis: University of Minnesota).

Space does not permit reference to the recent developments of the philosophy of science in other countries, but the names of some new journals can at least be mentioned: *Methodos* (Italy); *Analisi* (Italy); *Sigma* (Italy); *Science of Thought* (Japan, and in Japanese); *British Journal for the Philosophy of Science*. The *Revue internationale de philosophie* devoted a special issue to logical empiricism (Vol. IV [1950]). There are articles by B. Russell, R. Carnap, C. G. Hempel, H. Feigl, and M. Barzin; and a selected bibliography of 216 items prepared by H. Feigl. There has just been received a book by V. Kraft, *Der Wiener Kreis: Der Ursprung des Neopositivismus* (Wien: Springer, 1950).

The Institute for the Unity of Science was incorporated in 1949 with Philipp Frank, of Harvard University, as president of the Board of Trustees. A grant from the Rockefeller Foundation made this incorporation possible. The *International Encyclopedia of Unified Science* will henceforth be owned and directed by the Institute for the Unity of Science. The Institute has been furnished quarters by the American Academy of Arts and Sciences, 28 Newbury Street, Boston 16, Massachusetts.